"This marvelous book testified twice to the power
of personal integrity, determination, and courage. Its subject,
Mae Bertha Carter, and its author, Constance Curry, are two of a kind—
women whose convictions and actions would not be denied."
—ANDREW YOUNG

"Constance Curry has crafted a history of novelistic texture
and emotion from the true front lines of the civil rights struggle. . . .
This is a book teeming with loud voices and heat and faith, and
backbreaking work and timeless courage and honor."
—MELISSA FAYE GREENE

"*Silver Rights* deserves a place of honor
in the literature of the civil rights movement."
—HODDING CARTER III

"We sometimes forget what prices were paid to defeat
segregation. . . . Curry reminds us all with this moving account. . . .
It's an important document and an inspiring story."
—VERNON JORDAN

Silver Rights

Silver Rights

Constance Curry

WITH AN INTRODUCTION BY
MARIAN WRIGHT EDELMAN

A HARVEST BOOK
HARCOURT, INC.
San Diego   New York   London

Title page photograph: Pemble Plantation, 1965.
Map appearing on page x illustrated by Bill Nelson.

Abraham, Martin and John by Richard Holler. © 1968, 1970
Regent Music Corporation. Used by permission. All rights reserved.

This Harvest edition published by arrangement with Algonquin Books of Chapel Hill, a division of Workman Publishing.

Library of Congress Cataloging-in-Publication Data
Curry, Constance, 1933–
Silver rights/Constance Curry; with an introduction by Marian Wright Edelman.
p.   cm.—(A Harvest book)
Originally published: Chapel Hill, NC: Algonquin Books of Chapel Hill, 1995.
ISBN 0-15-600479-8
1. Afro-Americans—Mississippi—Sunflower County—Biography.
2. Carter family. 3. School integration—Mississippi—Sunflower County
(Miss.)—Race relations.   I. Title.
[F347.S9C87   1996]
976.2'4700496073—dc20   96-19289

Design by Bonnie Campbell
Text set in Palatino
Printed in the United States of America
First Harvest edition 1996
K J I H G F E D C

To the unsung heroes of the 1960s Civil Rights Movement who risked their lives and livelihoods to secure a better education for their children, and to the memory of my parents, Hazle and Ernest Curry.

Although I value the Civil Rights Movement *deeply*, I have never liked the term itself. It has no music, it has no poetry. It makes one think of bureaucrats rather than of sweaty faces, eyes bright and big for *Freedom!*, marching feet. . . . Older black country people did their best to instill what *accurate* poetry they could into this essentially white civil servants' term . . . so that what one *heard* was *"Silver."*

—Alice Walker, *In Search of Our Mothers' Gardens*

Contents

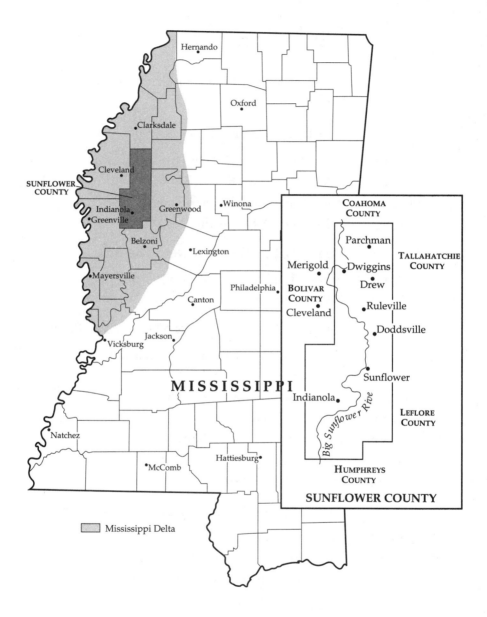

SUNFLOWER
COUNTY

Hernando

Oxford

Clarksdale

Cleveland

Winona

Indianola
Greenville

Greenwood

Belzoni

Lexington

Mayersville

Philadelphia

Canton

Jackson

Vicksburg

MISSISSIPPI

Natchez

McComb

Hattiesburg

Mississippi Delta

COAHOMA
COUNTY

Parchman

TALLAHATCHIE
COUNTY

Merigold

Dwiggins

Drew

BOLIVAR
COUNTY

Ruleville

Cleveland

Doddsville

Sunflower

Indianola

Big Sunflower River

LEFLORE
COUNTY

HUMPHREYS
COUNTY

SUNFLOWER COUNTY

Introduction

M ississippi . . . 1965. That's all you need to say to conjure up a portrait of the incredible individual struggles that made up a movement that forever changed our country. Many of those struggles are a part of history now, to be read and, I hope, appreciated by generations to come. Many of those individual struggles will never make it into our history books, but they are a part of our history nevertheless. I am grateful that one of my heroines has had her story brought to a wider audience by a wonderful author who was there to watch it unfold. Constance Curry was a member of the American Friends Service Committee (AFSC) and did all she could to help the Carter family in those years. Thank God for her, and for the Carters, and for those like them.

Mae Bertha and Matthew Carter and their family endured a terrifying nightmare to educate their children. They were the first (and only, for several years) black citizens in Sunflower County to sign Mississippi's "freedom of choice" papers, sending their children to previously all-white schools.

According to Title VI of the Civil Rights Act of 1964, Mississippi had to find a way to integrate its schools. "Freedom of choice" papers, to be signed by parents designating the schools their children would attend, were Mississippi's answer to avoiding desegregation. The white establishment knew black citizens could be intimidated and threatened and, one way or another, prevented from enrolling their children in the "white" schools.

Miss Mae Bertha and her family proved them wrong, just like the other brave band of parents who had dared challenge school segregation in *Brown v. Board of Education* to give their children a better future.

In June 1967, as an attorney with the NAACP Legal Defense and Educational Fund, I brought suit for Mae Bertha Carter on behalf of seven of her children, Larry, Stanley, Gloria, Pearl, Beverly, Deborah, and Carl, against the Drew, Mississippi, Municipal Separate School District in U.S. District Court. In that suit we stated that the "fear of white retaliation, firmly grounded in fact, has deterred other Negroes from choosing the formerly white schools pursuant to the district's freedom of choice plan." The class-action suit asked for injunctive relief against the segregated and discriminatory system that placed a "cruel and intolerable burden" upon black parents and students. We won. The court decision came down in 1969 throwing out "freedom of choice" plans and ordering desegregation of the schools. That could not have happened without the Carters.

Miss Mae Bertha and her husband Matthew joined the NAACP in 1955, slipping quietly into secret meetings in the churches. It was a dangerous thing to be a member of the NAACP in Mississippi in 1955. In the sixties and seventies she and her family spoke out and marched. Two Carter daughters were arrested for marching for voting rights. Miss Mae Bertha and Matthew were part of the 1 percent of the black population in Mississippi who registered to vote when the Voting Rights Act passed in 1965.

This deeply moving book chronicles the pain and poverty in the lives of sharecroppers, their extraordinary grit, courage, and endurance. Miss Mae Bertha's children had listened to their great-grandmother tell stories of being a slave and to their grandmother talk of freezing winters without wood and nothing but last summer's dried vegetables to eat. The older Carter children spent backbreaking days picking cotton, went to poor all-black schools that operated only part of the school year, shared old school buses, old books, and precious few supplies. All-black schools of the time were sometimes taught by teachers who had limited educations themselves. When the opportunity came for the eight younger Carter children to go to better schools, the Carters stood united, children and parents, in their determination to ensure a better future, no matter what the cost. Miss Mae Bertha said that changing schools was the chance to get the children out of the cotton fields. The whole family felt that it was the right thing to do. The older children signed their own freedom of choice papers and Miss Mae Bertha signed for the younger ones.

Every day Miss Mae Bertha struggled to maintain her courage, commitment, and perseverance to achieve and obtain what was right for herself and her children. She never lost sight of the goal: getting the best education possible for her children.

Equally as important, her work didn't stop with her own children. After taking a job with Head Start and working with young children, she continued to work on school desegregation and the second generation of problems resulting from school desegregation—disproportionate suspensions of black male students, different conduct rules for black students (including a demerit system that included sneezing as an offense), and overinclusion in special education programs.

In 1969, Miss Mae Bertha traveled with other civil rights activists to Washington, D.C., on a trip sponsored by the AFSC. They went to see then-Attorney General John Mitchell and occupied his office when he refused to see them. There, as always, her message was clear and powerful—she was there as a black mother who wanted the best for her children. She was not talking about why blacks should go to school with whites; she knew access to a better education and a better life for her children was the prize. The attorney general finally relented and saw them, but she was ready to go to jail if necessary for her principles and her right to be heard.

She continued her voter registration work and later helped form and became president of the Drew Improvement Association. She worked with parents and children in the town to keep up the pressure and the interest in better education for all children. She has served as a vice president of the NAACP and her daughter Beverly has served on the formerly all-white school board that so resisted the Carter children's enrollment years ago.

When Connie Curry interviewed Miss Mae Bertha's now-grown children for this book, they talked about those days: the spitballs, the epithets, the mistreatment and fear, and the way they tried not to return hatred for hatred. Their mother was always there for the children, listening, helping them talk it out. The only things she wouldn't let them say were that they hated all whites or that they wished they'd never been born. Ruth, the eldest daughter to desegregate the schools, said to Connie, "Mama was right about hate, because you don't feel good about yourself when you hate someone else." Imagine all they were faced with, and imagine the strength it took not to hate.

Children learn what they are taught. Perhaps the cruelty of the white children can be forgiven because, sadly, and unlike Miss Mae Bertha's children, they were taught by their parents and white community leaders and elders to hate. More difficult to forgive was the unspeakable cruelty from teachers and principals to the Carter children. Daughter Deborah told Connie about a white girl who wanted to befriend her in grammar school. This meant so much because everybody else treated her as a social leper. When the principal saw them together at recess, he ordered the white girl not to associate with Deborah.

In a letter written to Connie at the time, Miss Mae Bertha described ten-year-old Pearl's teacher, who frequently told Pearl that she smelled and that she should take a bath and put on clean clothes. Having bathed and put clean clothes on Pearl every morning before she left for school, Miss Mae Bertha wrote, "I think the teacher is cracking up."

Classes were told to go to the public library to check out books. But the Carter children were not allowed a library card unless they had a "reference," a man of substance in the town who would sign for them. Of course, this was impossible. When they asked if they could study in the library, they were told that the library was "too small."

Pearl described to Connie the years when only her brothers and sisters and herself desegregated the schools as "years of hell." But never did the children waver in their determination to stick it out, to get through it somehow, and to get an education. Eight Carter children graduated from Drew, the so-called "white" high school, and seven went on to college at Ole Miss.

Daughter Gloria, now a corporate vice president with an M.B.A., remembers the harassments and the pain. But she told Connie: "We never once thought of quitting. We were not going to let them run us away." She added, though, "Up until a few years ago, I was still having nightmares about being in Drew High School, and I would wake up sobbing."

Miss Mae Bertha tried to convince other black families to enroll their children in Drew's "white" schools. None did. I can't blame them. But how deeply I admire the courage of the Carters and all those throughout the South who challenged the white establishment in those years!

Matthew Carter died in 1988, leaving a great hole in his family and community. But his wife continues to fight the good fight. In 1993, she was one of six African-Americans to receive the University of Mississippi's annual Award of Distinction.

Miss Mae Bertha was and is a woman of deep faith. Throughout all the personal and family ordeals and dangers, she prayed and believed in her "protective covering," God's blessing and protection. Her willingness to take enormous risks stemmed partly from this unshrinking faith and partly from her determination as a loving mother to do whatever was necessary to give her children the best possible lives.

Her wisdom, strength, and absolute commitment to making justice real in the world serve as a beacon to parents today who want to do the right thing for their children despite enormous obstacles. Her courage and steely will inspire me as I look back and look forward to what we have to do as parents, communities, and a nation to leave no child behind. We desperately need inspiration now as the struggle continues: against poor education, prejudice, greed, government short-sightedness, and penny-wise/pound-foolish economic policies robbing our children of their future.

Come to know Miss Mae Bertha Carter and her family in these pages and hold them in your heart. As we face many new challenges, let us ask God to grant us her "protective covering," her grace, and her courage.

I thank Connie Curry for sharing this great life with us. Together we must pick up where the Carter parents and children left off after cracking the ugly face of legal apartheid in Sunflower County, Mississippi, and America. We must together build a powerful movement to put the social and economic underpinnings under every child by ensuring them a Healthy Start, a Head Start, a Fair Start, a Safe Start, and a Moral Start in life with the support of caring parents and communities.

Marian Wright Edelman
President, Children's Defense Fund
Washington, D.C.

Preface

*T*he U.S. Civil Rights Act of 1964 ordered desegregation of all public schools receiving federal aid. To comply, many southern school districts drew up "freedom of choice" plans that supposedly permitted all parents, black and white, to send their children to the schools of their choice. It was a cruel hoax, a ruse by white segregationists who assumed that blacks, dependent on whites for work and a place to live, would never dare choose "white" schools for their children.

But Lyndon Johnson had promised to uphold the law of the land, and some African-American parents, trusting the president's words, did exercise their freedom of choice and enrolled their children in previously all-white school systems. What happened to these families is an untold story and, for some, a tragic one. For others it is a story of sacrifice and struggle but eventually of success.

THE CARTER family and its forebears had been sharecropping on various plantations in the Mississippi Delta for more than sixty years. By 1965 little had changed. Matthew and Mae Bertha Carter were "cropping" twenty-five acres of land on the Pemble Plantation, nine miles from the tiny cotton town of Drew, Mississippi, in the middle of Sunflower County, in the heart of the Mississippi Delta.

Matthew and Mae Bertha had been married since 1939. Altogether their *family included thirteen children—a family that size was considered an asset in cotton country. It meant thirty hands, including their own, to chop and pick the crop. The Carters' five oldest children—Edna, Bertha, Naomi, Matthew, and John—had attended "Negro schools" that operated on a split-session schedule, according to the cotton crop's needs. School began in December or January, stopped in the early spring—"chopping time"—resumed in the broiling summer months, and turned out again in September and October— "picking time." As each of the five oldest Carter children graduated from high school, they went north, the young men to the armed services and the women to find work or to live with relatives.*

But there were still eight children at home, and on August 12, 1965, Mae Bertha and Matthew became the first (and for two years the only) black parents to enroll their children in the previously all-white schools in Drew, Mississippi. Ruth, Larry, Gloria, and Stanley desegregated Drew High School; Pearl, Beverly, and Deborah desegregated the A. W. James Elementary School. Carl was only a toddler, still too young for school; he would not join the desegration effort until 1967.

I FIRST met the Carters at their home on the Pemble Plantation in January 1966. I was the southern field representative for the American Friends Service Committee (AFSC), a Quaker organization. My job was to investigate reports of intimidation and reprisals against black families like the Carters that were attempting to desegregate the schools under Title VI of the Civil Rights Act of 1964. I visited the Carters many times between 1966 and 1975, and my assignment included helping them find a house in Drew, locating jobs for Matthew and Mae Bertha, and ensuring fair treatment for the children. I left the American Friends Service Committee to become the director of human services for the city of Atlanta in 1975 and lost track of the Carters until 1988, when, at a conference in Atlanta on Women in the Civil Rights Movement, I ran into Mae Bertha. I could barely believe my eyes when I looked across the room just before the opening session and saw her. Even after thirteen years we recognized each other immediately and ran to hug each other as if there had been no passage of time at all.

I returned to Mississippi in May 1989 to interview Mae Bertha for the American Friends Service Committee as part of an oral history project. It was twenty-five years, almost to the day, since I had first set foot in Mississippi. The feelings and the memories rushed in once again as I drove through the green lushness of the Delta toward Drew. In trying to describe the Mississippi Delta, I seem to find only superlatives—the flattest land, the blackest dirt, the hottest summers, the nicest people, the poorest people. In defining the Delta's past and even its present, I am aware of these extremes and also of its incongruities: the violence and the peacefulness, the beauty and the ugliness, the stillness and the tension. It is a place complex almost beyond comprehension.

Such contrasts mark the Delta landscape, and not all important moments in its history are commemorated by metal plaques along the roadside. The most inconspicuous patches of land, tumbledown barns, and innocuous storefronts have been the scenes of both great tragedy and great heroism. Each time I went back to Mississippi to do more research for the oral history project, Mae Bertha and I would get in my car and ride around Sunflower County. On one of our drives we passed through land that once had been part of the Birch Plantation. Mae Bertha's mother, Luvenia Slaughter, lived on Birch Plantation until she married in 1919. On other drives, Mae Bertha pointed out still more landmarks—the barn just outside Drew where Emmett Till was supposedly murdered, the porch of an old house where Charley Patton used to sit and play and sing the blues before he became famous, the section of Drew called Crocker's Cypress Canebrake, where in the 1930s black dayworkers lived and where dancing, music, and card playing were provided them while the white owner ran other whites off with his gun.

I have listened for many hours to Mae Bertha's stories. I have interviewed all thirteen of her children, many of her thirty-two grandchildren, and some of her seventeen great-grandchildren. K.C. Moore, Matthew Carter's cousin, told me stories about life on Widow Belle Parker's plantation where he and Matthew grew up. I also interviewed many other people in Sunflower County, black and white, who were part of the Carter story or who remember hearing pieces of it. When I visited Mae Bertha's mother, Luvenia, who is now ninety-two and lives in Toledo, Ohio, I realized that to understand the Carters' courage in a place like Drew, Luvenia's story should also be told. The threads in the fabric of the Carters' lives stretch back to the early part of the century, when Matthew's and Mae Bertha's parents and grandparents share-cropped in Sunflower County and dreamed of ways to free their children from that oppressive way of life.

In 1955, when a young black minister "writing people up for the NAACP" approached Mae Bertha and Matthew, Mae Bertha said to him, "Advancement for colored people! We're for that. Sign us up." That decision, the arrival of young civil rights workers in the Delta, the inspiration in mass meetings and freedom songs, and the incarceration of Ruth and Naomi Carter at the Jackson, Mississippi, fairgrounds during a march to support the proposed Voting Rights Act—all are tightly woven into the Carter family history. But the Carters' story—choosing the white schools, struggling against ongoing harassment and racism—continues long after the passage of the Voting Rights Act in 1965 and the Meredith March on the roads of Mississippi in 1966—the two events traditionally recognized by civil rights chroniclers as the end of the freedom movement. And into the full fabric of the movement must also be woven the lives of the hundreds of other black families across the South that, like the Carters, risked everything to provide a better future for their children. Many black parents signed the freedom of choice papers to integrate schools but withdrew their children in the face of organized intimidation. The American Friends Service Committee Family Aid Fund helped approximately one hundred families withstand the threats, stay in their communities, and keep their children in the white schools. But there were many other families we never knew.

In the earliest years of school desegregation, in cities like Little Rock and New Orleans, where integration was imposed by court order, blacks had the benefit of community support, federal protection, and widespread media coverage. But for the Carters and so many other families in the rural South, there were no federal troops to guard them and no reporters to tell the stories of their suffering. They not only faced danger from the white community but very often rejection by the black community as well. Abandoned by the federal government and forgotten by the American people, their children went to the white schools anyway.

THE MISSISSIPPI Delta, two hundred miles long and seventy miles across at its widest point, is a diamond-shaped expanse of flat land stretching southwest from Memphis, Tennessee, to Vicksburg, Mississippi. Over the course of centuries, the unpredictable and uncontrollable Mississippi River flood waters deposited the sediment that makes up the legendary dark, rich alluvial soil of the Delta and produced a vast swampy wilderness of vines, cane, brush, and trees. In those early days, panthers and bears lived in the forests. Flooding from the river and fever from the insects caused severe health problems for early settlers who ventured into the dense swamps and forests. An eighteenth-century scholar described the Delta as a *"lush, seething hell." As the wilderness was slowly tamed and as stronger levees were built to hold back the river, the Delta took on a new life. A cotton-plantation economy developed with strict rules on how its inhabitants should live, and the fortunes of its people, white and black, master and slave, were inextricably bound together.*

Mississippi was admitted to the Union in 1817 as the twentieth state. Sunflower County was created in 1844 from an eastern slice of Bolivar County, and its boundaries fluctuated thereafter as it gained and lost pieces of adjoining counties until its present boundaries were established in 1918. A thin finger of land in almost the exact geographical center of the Delta, the county is forty-nine miles from north to south and stretches eighteen miles at its widest point. The Sunflower, Quiver, and Hushpuckena rivers drain the county, and the Sunflower, the largest river, curves and twists for a journey of one hundred miles.

Excavations have shown that in the thirteenth century predecessors of the Choctaw and Chickasaw tribes lived and thrived in Sunflower County. The sixteenth and seventeenth centuries brought European explorers and missionaries, along with smallpox, measles and venereal diseases—plagues that, along with colonial violence, decimated the Native-American population. The treaties of Doaks' Stand in 1820 and Dancing Rabbit Creek in 1830 arranged for the removal of Native Americans across the Mississippi River to a reservation; by 1890 only four Native Americans were listed in the census for Sunflower County.

Settling the Delta was daunting, since draining marshes and swamps and clearing virgin forests and canebrakes required phenomenal labor. Workers faced intense heat, insect-borne fevers, wild animals, isolation, and loneliness. Nevertheless, land speculation increased in Sunflower in the 1830s and the price of an acre soared during the next thirty years as the burgeoning slave population pushed back the forests and prepared the land for cotton. In 1848, there were 616 slaves in the county. By 1860, almost 4,000 of the 5,000 inhabitants were slaves.

So outnumbered, the whites lived in constant fear of slave insurrection. In 1849, the first hanging in the county was recorded when the murder of the slaveowner Robert Beverly by his houseboy led to the execution of six slaves: whites treated the affair as a slave uprising. The court compensated Beverly's son to the tune of $5,251 for the loss of his six slaves.

The Civil War interrupted the sale of the land and temporarily halted growth. Following the war, landowners returned from the Confederate army to rebuild their homes and replant their fields, but with little money and no slaves. To add to their difficulties, a flood in 1867 destroyed Delta farmlands and levees along the Mississippi River. Particularly galling to them were their former slaves. Under Reconstruction, blacks in Sunflower County held the offices of sheriff, superintendent of education, and county supervisor. Two black men served as president pro tem of the board of supervisors in 1872, and the first grand jury to serve that year was almost equally divided between whites and blacks.

The Ku Klux Klan ruthlessly employed violence and intimidation against the freedmen. Eventually southern white resistance and the depression of 1873 sapped the political will of the federal government. Reconstruction collapsed. Its end was marked in Sunflower County when, in 1876, the majority-white board of supervisors declared vacant the offices held by blacks. The positions were then filled by whites. Nearly a century later, a second reconstruction would run up against the same kind of vehement resistance.

In the 1880s, after the federal government had funded the rebuilding of the levees and as railroad expansion brought in people and supplies, Sunflower's economy flourished again. In that boom market, companies and individuals from outside the Delta bought many massive land parcels. By the turn of the century, a wealthy elite of white planters, both absentee and in residence, rested securely on the shoulders of the sharecroppers who raised their cotton.

Sharecropping originated as a rough compromise between white land-owners and former slaves, but it soon evolved into a system of semi-slavery. Landowners needed an enormous labor force to produce cotton, but most did not have ready cash to pay wages; blacks wanted to work in family units rather than in gangs under white foremen. Landowners thus offered twenty to forty acres of farmland to a sharecropper and extended him credit for food, seed, fertilizer, and other necessities. According to law, the entire crop belonged to the landowner, and at the end of the growing season—"settle-ment time"—the landowner would calculate the amount earned from sale of the cotton and then subtract both the sharecropper's rent and his debt for sup-plies bought on credit from the plantation store or commissary. With no access to the sales negotiations and no way to check the amount of credit extended to them, sharecroppers were at the mercy of the planters. Most sharecroppers remained in constant debt; some even found themselves in peonage, with their landlords forcibly preventing them from leaving the plan-tation. As demand for cotton increased at the turn of the century, 80 percent of the population in Sunflower County was black, and it provided the labor force on the plantations to meet that ravenous demand.

The stage was set for small battles that would change the balance of power in the Delta forever. This is the story of one Delta family's own battle to make those changes happen—to seek justice.

PEOPLE UNINHIBITED *by the conventions of formal education often take unfamiliar expressions and translate them into phrases more meaningful to them. Oftentimes the new term contains a pleasing or beautiful image.*

Working as I did with Mississippi families in rural areas, I came to think of what they were fighting for as they did—as their "silver rights." The writer Alice Walker has also observed that the term civil *rights "has no music, it has no poetry. It makes one think of bureaucrats rather than of sweaty faces, eyes bright and big for* freedom!, *marching feet." Silver rights, silver rights, indeed. Like the metal, the dreams the Carter family and many others sought were bright, shining, and precious.*

Constance Curry
Atlanta, Georgia
March 1995

Mae Bertha Carter and author, 1994.

Part I
Choices

Mae Bertha Carter, 1969.

The Carter children ready for school, fall 1965. Left to right: Gloria, Pearl, Deborah, Larry, Beverly, Stanley, Ruth.

One

We Thought They Meant It

G o back to your own schools, niggers," hollered white hecklers standing along the streets. It was the first day of the 1965 school year in the cotton town of Drew, Mississippi. The crowd shouted and shook angry fists at seven black children just visible at the windows of a big yellow school bus.

Inside the bus, sixteen-year-old Ruth Carter sat in a seat by herself and watched the crowd outside. She couldn't hear their words but she saw their faces. She also watched her four younger sisters and two younger brothers sitting in front of her, scared stiff, eyes round and

3

staring straight ahead. Ruth knew that she bore the heaviest burden in the children's decision to go to the white schools. She hated the cotton fields more than any of the other children. And more than the others she had resented the split sessions of the black schools and the shiny buses that whizzed past carrying the white children to school for nine whole months each year. She knew why they were on the bus that morning but it didn't help her overcome the terror she now faced. She hadn't realized they would be the only ones—the only black children to board the bus, the only black children to walk up the steps and through the doors of the white schools.

Just days before school was scheduled to begin, a memo from the director of the Federal Bureau of Investigation to the FBI office in Jackson, Mississippi, had ordered special attention to the town of Drew. A return memo to Washington on August 27, 1965, confirmed that Jackson agents would observe the first day of school in Drew on September 3. FBI agents interviewed Drew police and other civic leaders and told them that the investigation was being conducted at the specific request of John Doar, assistant attorney general of the Civil Rights Division, U.S. Department of Justice.

On the morning that school opened, Sunflower County Deputy Sheriff John Sidney Parker stationed two cars, with four men in each, where they could escort one particular school bus once it turned off a cotton-plantation road onto the highway to Drew. The city police and several FBI agents met the bus at the city limits and followed it to Drew High School and then on to A. W. James Elementary School. At both schools, policemen stood along the sidewalks and in the doorways until the seven black children were safely inside, in the principal's office. These precautions were taken every day for a week until it was deemed that the arrival of the children, all sons and daughters of Matthew and Mae Bertha Carter, had settled into a "normal" routine.

On September 7, the FBI reported to Washington that "seven Negro children registered to attend formerly white schools in Drew, Miss. Local authorities do not intend to have violation of the law on the part of anyone. The children attended school opening day without incident." This report to J. Edgar Hoover, and the modest show of force at school opening, was the extent of the FBI's involvement. Once inside the school, the Carter children faced the spitballs, name-calling, ostracism, and unceasing harassment they would endure for the next four years.

ENTERING THE Mississippi Delta is like turning the page in a picture book. In an instant, the rolling highway gives way to land that is perfectly level. Traveling a road—a flatter than flat wet blacktop, straight as a ruler, heading north from Yazoo City on Highway 49 East—at midday on January 16, 1966, Winifred Green was at the wheel and I was in the passenger seat of her green '65 Volkswagen bug. The radio dial was tuned to WCLD, our favorite country music station. Outside, as far as the eye could see, there was nothing but row after row of bare brown cotton plants. The soil was very black. Here and there stray wisps of cotton clung to the stems, the only whiteness in the uninterrupted gray-brown landscape of winter fields. Clumps of ancient cypress trees on the horizon defined the banks of the bayous.

The white pickup I saw in my side mirror had been following us since we turned left onto a smaller road into Sunflower County. In the truck's cab were two white men wearing hunting caps.

"Winifred," I said, "can you see? Is there a gun in the rack?"

"There's a gun in the rack," she said.

We figured that under those hunting caps their thoughts were something like, "There go two white girls in an out-of-state car, driving through the cotton fields looking to stir up trouble with the coloreds."

Winifred was a native Mississippian and she knew the drill. She said to me, "If they start to pass, scrunch down low in your seat."

"Wait," I said. "I think this is the road. Turn left here." I checked my directions. "Maybe they won't follow us."

They didn't, mercifully, but we soon realized we were at a dead end, lost on a muddy one-lane road—really just a path widened by tractors and sprayers and cotton-pickers. The fields surrounded us, and this little road through them was so narrow the car door grazed the dead cotton plants when I got out to look around. I was worried and tired. I had flown that morning to Jackson, Mississippi, from my home in Atlanta to meet Winifred, my coworker with the American Friends Service Committee, and to drive the hundred or so miles north into the Delta. Our assignment in Sunflower County was to visit Matthew and Mae Bertha Carter. By the time we finally found their house it was midafternoon.

The sharecropper house, covered with imitation-brick siding worn to weather-beaten pink, had been assigned to the Carters when they moved to Pemble's plantation in 1956. Matthew and Mae Bertha had decided to leave the tenant plot at Tom Rushing's place, where they had been working for five years, because their family was growing and they needed a bigger share and a bigger house. T. E. Pemble was hiring on a place closer to Drew. Over the years, Pemble had acquired many acres of land in Sunflower and Bolivar counties. He owned a cotton gin and a retail store in Merigold and was known in the black community as a good person to work for.

The Carters' house was on Busyline, another narrow dirt road running between cotton fields. Busyline was so named because it gave main access to two paved roads, one at its north end that went from Drew to Merigold and the other at its south end that went from Drew to Renova, where it intersected with Highway 61, the route to Cleveland, Mississippi.

The Carters' house had five rooms and eleven doors. A long porch ran all the way across the front. Two doors opened from the porch into two front rooms, one a living room and the other a bedroom with two double beds, a dresser, and wooden shelves on one wall. In the living room, company visited and boyfriends came to court the Carter girls. There were propane gas stoves for heat in the living room and front bedroom. The long room behind the two front rooms held two more double beds. Matthew and Mae Bertha slept in one of them with their youngest child. Two of the children slept in the other bed. This back room also housed the dining room table and chairs, some trunks for clothes, and the refrigerator. A small kitchen with a wood stove and a metal tub was built onto the back room. The metal tub was for washing clothes and for bathing. Water was brought in from a pump in the backyard near the animal pen, but the pump water yellowed the containers, so Matthew hauled drinking water from a well about a mile away.

Following the births of Beverly in 1957 and Deborah in 1959, an abandoned shack had been dragged by tractor and attached to the back of the house to make the fifth room, a bedroom for Larry and Stanley, the two older sons.

A six-by-six garden patch to the left of the porch was winter-deadened when we saw it that January. The Carters depended on its summer yield, which Mae Bertha would can for the winter. Farther down the road and to the left was a big, weathered wood barn that housed the plantation's tractors and heavy farm equipment. The fields behind the barn included one acre on which the Carters planted corn and other crops for their own use.

A few rosebushes grew in a patch to the right of the front porch. It was Mae Bertha's flower garden. Each summer Matthew filled it with her favorites—burning bushes and four-o'clocks. In back of the house was the smokehouse and an enclosure for the pigs, mules, and cows. The pen for the chickens was in the backyard behind the kitchen. Farther back was the outhouse.

On that cold, bleak afternoon, Mae Bertha and Matthew were on the porch to meet us. Mae Bertha, all of five feet two, was light skinned, almost almond colored. Her blue eyes, then as now, seemed to disappear when her face crinkled in laughter. She wore a print gingham dress and a blue sweater and held her youngest, four-year-old Carl, in her arms.

"I've been praying for your safe arrival," she said. "I'm so glad to see you." Setting Carl down on his feet, she took our hands in hers and then gave each of us a big hug.

Matthew was just slightly taller than his wife, and his gentle face much darker than hers. He wore khaki pants and, cold as it was, a short-sleeved blue shirt. He shook our hands and led us across the front porch into the sparsely furnished living room. I remember looking through a hole in the porch floor and seeing a yellow dog and a calico cat curled together for protection from the winter cold.

The Carters offered Winifred and me seats on the worn living room couch. The walls of the room were papered in a faded blue and yellow flower pattern, and over a small wooden table against the wall to our right hung two color photographs, one of President John F. Kennedy and the other of Dr. Martin Luther King, Jr. The floors were bare, and blue plastic curtains hung at the two windows. Mae Bertha sat in the only other chair in the room. Matthew pulled in a dining room chair from the back room.

I could smell turnip greens cooking and wished I knew the Carters well enough to ask for a bowl. We were always hungry on these field trips; we often spent hours searching for our destination and usually our only option for food was a gas station for Cokes and cheese crackers. As the southern field representative for the AFSC, I was visiting black families in the Delta who had reportedly suffered reprisals after enrolling their children in previously all-white public schools under the Civil Rights Act of 1964. Jean Fairfax, the director of southern programs for the Community Relations Division at the AFSC national office in Philadelphia, had visited the Carters herself in November and asked that Winifred and I visit them in January. We were there to find out how things were going.

What they told us that day was as bleak as the Delta's winter landscape. Matthew sat quietly and listened with an occasional nod of assent as his wife described some of what had happened since September. A born storyteller, she related her tale brilliantly, imitating everyone involved, from FBI agents to the plantation overseer.

She told us how one moonless night in November someone had torn down their animal pens and how the cows and pigs were never recovered. She told us how for ten years the family had been allowed to follow behind the automatic cotton-picking machines that came through their twenty-five acres in late fall, so that the family could pick the fields completely clean to make a few more bales for itself. But that past fall, a disk attached to the picker had plowed all the final cotton under. She told us how when Matthew had gone for his settlement on December 10, the overseer told him he was ninety-seven dollars in debt, that there was no more land for him to work, and that the family would have to move out as soon as Matthew found another place. (The owner's son-in-law explained to outsiders that the Carters had to move because the plantation's cotton allotment had been cut—"it had nothing to do with that school business.")

When Mae Bertha paused, Matthew moved his chair a little closer to us and told us that John Lyon from the U.S. Justice Department had been down to visit on January 13 and that he and Mae Bertha had told him the whole story, too. Winifred and I looked at each other. So the barrage of letters and complaints to the Justice Department from the AFSC the previous fall *had* had an effect. In the two years that Winifred and I had worked for the AFSC, hard evidence of the success of the organization's lobbying efforts had been rare; this news was especially sweet.

Mae Bertha spoke again, more softly. "The children are doing well in school after four months and they want to stay," she told us, "but things are just so hard. You know, though, I never had the opportunity to go to a real school. The only school I can remember going to was the church house where we all went about three months in the year. And the teacher, she had to teach all the kids at the school coming from different plantations around there. Sometimes she would have forty to fifty kids to teach and she had to teach all subjects."

Mae Bertha continued, "And I'd say she was about fourth grade in her own education, because I wanted to learn about fractions and she didn't know how and every time we would get to that, she would always skip it. She could teach adding and subtracting but she didn't know the fractions and she would just touch a little on all those subjects so I didn't really get the chance to go to a real school. So, I always said if I ever got any kids—that would be my goal—to send them to school. I figure I went up to about the fifth grade. I learned some, but some of it I learned by experience and reading and trying to write and some from television and listening and then what comes from other peoples you experience."

Matthew, whose own schooling had ended in the third grade, also wanted more for his children, and he believed the only way to get it was through education. I asked him why they had enrolled their children in the white school in the first place. He looked me right in the eye, opened his hands in his lap, and said simply, "We thought they meant it."

He and Mae Bertha believed the Drew school board's letter instructing parents to send their children to the school of their choice. They believed that the new laws would provide their children with the same educational opportunities provided to the white children of Sunflower County.

Matthew repeated to me what he always told his kids: "When you are black and uneducated, ain't nothing you can do. You're just handicapped. If we hadn't been handicapped, we wouldn't still be on these plantations working for nothing. We stay and stay out there, and we don't have no authority over nothing that we're growing. The man, he always sells the cotton we grow and he don't never bring us no bill of sale. We can't tell *him* what we owe him. He always tells *us* what we owe him. Then at settlement time, he tells us what we got out of our cotton."

Winifred and I leaned closer to him as he continued in his gentle, quiet voice. "The man would say, 'Well you did pretty good but you've still got some cotton out in the field and that's going to bring you some money. So get that picked out and then maybe you'll have a little more.' But we never see no little more."

Matthew told us that although most of the families on the surrounding plantations stopped picking cotton at noon each Friday and didn't pick again until Monday morning, it was not so for the Carter family. When the cotton was ready for picking, the Carters picked from Monday morning until Saturday night. They picked from "can to can't," until the light failed or the weather interfered. "Can't" rarely included physical exhaustion or illness.

Matthew told the children, "Don't pay attention to the people who go home at Friday noon. When school starts, they'll be waving at you from the field and you'll be riding the bus." And that's what happened. With most of the family working, the Carters were able to pick three bales of cotton a week and often another bale in the extra weekend time. When school started, any cotton left in the fields got picked in the late afternoon after the children came home.

Mae Bertha and Matthew had little time to tell us about their lives that first day. But over the years of our friendship I learned a great deal about what it was like for black sharecropping families trying to subsist on a big Mississippi cotton plantation.

As on other plantations, life along Busyline stretched into rows of cotton fields with an inevitability barely stirred by an Emmett Till lynching or a Supreme Court decision. Every morning at picking time, no matter what, the older children and Matthew and Mae Bertha went to the cotton fields. Everybody wore pants and long-sleeved shirts and old shoes with the backs cut out for some protection from the burning ground. After a rain, they put on boots, picked cotton to where the plants were practically underwater, and then moved to a higher, drier part of the field. For each child big enough to chop or pick cotton, every single day revolved around the needs of the crop. No matter what.

The Carters' two oldest sons—John Caesar, known as J.C., and Matthew, nicknamed Man—had started picking when they were three years old, just able to carry little flour sacks that they would fill with cotton and then empty into their parents' hundred-pound sacks to be weighed by the overseer later in the day. When he was a little older, Man would also go into the fields at night if the family was behind in picking. He often filled a hundred-pound sack by moonlight. Sometimes in the lonely fields sprinkled with silver cotton blooms he would see an airplane from nearby Greenville Air Force Base. As he watched it, momentarily silhouetted against the moon and then disappearing into the dark sky, he dreamed that someday he would fly an airplane, "free up there—far away from the cotton fields." When he was eighteen years old, Man joined the air force, became a pilot, and remained in the service until he retired in 1983 with the rank of senior master sergeant.

J.C. remembers picking cotton before he was old enough to go to school and being frightened one day by some wasps in the cotton stalks. "I could see them. And my dad kept telling me, 'Come on here, boy, you just don't want to pick that cotton.' And he got a switch and I got a whipping and then when he got to that cotton stalk, the wasps stung him up on his head.

"When it would come time for the cotton to make into the bolls," J.C. continued, "I would look up and down those fields, and I could practically feel them opening—millions and millions of white bolls—knowing you'd have to go out there and pick every last one of them. That was discouraging to me. And when you'd look across the field, you'd see the actual little heat waves running across the fields like little monkeys. That's what we would call those little heat waves—monkeys. Heat that you could actually see jumping, and millions of white bolls—nightmares.

"Later, maybe when I'm eight—I was picking cotton big time then—we moved to where a school started in September, but we usually picked in September, so I had to stay out of school. Then, when you get home in the evenings, first thing, 'How much cotton you pick?' from Mama. She'd say, 'Go bring me that switch,' and, 'Boy, when my brother was your age, he was picking a hundred pounds of cotton.'"

Before their own cotton was ready, or after it was already picked, the Carters would hire out to pick on the surrounding plantations at three dollars a day. Trucks picked up workers at designated stops, drove them to the fields to pick cotton all day, and then took them home. The one advantage of hiring out was the payment at the end of the day. Meager as the three dollars might be, it was at least a little cash in hand so that the family finances weren't entirely dependent on the annual settlement figured by the plantation bookkeepers.

All of the family worked until sundown, then the children helped with washing dishes, cleaning the house, and helping Matthew pump water for the mules. Most of the time the family had two mules, indispensable for pulling the plow. At Busyline, the family's favorite mule was named Bill. The day that Bill died, Mae Bertha's neighbor found her crying. "Well, I thank God it wasn't the children," Mae Bertha later told me. "We was blessed after all."

If there was still daylight when chores were done and supper was over, the children played ball in the yard with neighbors. Mae Bertha told her children stories whenever there was time, mostly in the winter when the evenings were long. The stories had been passed down from Mae Bertha's mother and grandmother. Some stories were short, and a lot of them made fun of preachers. "Preacher had his eye on a young lady in the congregation and was trying to get her husband out of the way. He asked the couple's little boy to come to church and sing a song: 'Daddy's been stealing preacher man's hogs and preacher don't even know it.' Boy practiced and practiced and then on the Sunday, he got up and sang, 'Preacher been sleepin' with Mommy every night and Daddy don't even know it.'"

Many nights when everyone else had gone to bed, Matthew stayed up late making panties for his daughters from cotton flour sacks. He sewed elastic at the waist, and when a pair wore out, he took the elastic out and laid the old pair down on some flour-sack cloth and cut out the new pair. A special treat was a flour sack with a flowered pattern. Mae Bertha could not sew as well and was thankful that Matthew had learned when helping his mother make quilts. With so many children, there were many hand-me-down items of clothing. Only occasionally were clothes bought from the store or made by other people.

Mae Bertha did have a cousin, Pearly, who would make dresses for the smaller girls. And she could do it overnight. They always were brightly colored and always had three ruffles. They were usually made for Easter and passed down to each successive sister. Sometimes just when Mae Bertha was wondering where badly needed shoes or clothing would come from, Cousin Pearly (who had a little more money than the Carters) would drive up with dresses. Mae Bertha named her daughter Pearl after her cousin.

On Sundays the Carters put on their best clothes for church. Preaching and singing lasted from eleven to one at Union Grove Baptist Church. Afterwards, Sunday dinner was freshly killed chicken, vegetables from the garden, sweet potato pies, and a caramel cake, or maybe a coconut cake with jelly filling. After dinner came work in the house or garden, so Sundays weren't much of a day off, but in the late afternoon neighbors would visit or the Carters would themselves go visiting. Everybody went back to church in the evening, since this was the main form of recreation and socializing.

The only real time off came during "lay-by" in the summer, when the family was waiting for the cotton to open. But even lay-by was spent picking and canning vegetables and putting food up for the winter. In the garden grew cabbage, greens, cucumbers, butter beans and pole beans, squash, white and sweet potatoes, corn, popcorn, tomatoes, okra, and peas. Mae Bertha canned anything that could go in a jar so that no matter the season there could be a big pot of gumbo soup.

In summer there were always berries to be picked on the creek banks, a job that Mae Bertha and the children liked. Apple and peach trees meant canned fruit for winter, at least until the plantation owners cut down the trees because they needed more land for growing cash crops. When the time was right, Matthew would go down to the melon patch and bring back cantaloupes and huge watermelons that were nearly ripe to put in the back room. He would tell the children that the melons wouldn't be ready for two more weeks. The children always laughed, because by the time he said that they had already started eating the melons.

But the favorite watermelons were the "volunteers," which somehow grew in the cotton rows. In late summer and early fall, when the heat, boredom, and fatigue of picking cotton would become nearly unbearable, there might appear at one's feet a big, thirst-quenching watermelon, still cold from the dew the night before. Mae Bertha says that such surprises are the reason that black people have traditionally loved watermelons.

Matthew also planned carefully so that he had hogs for meat and cows to provide milk and butter. He would kill the hogs in the fall and hang big hams in the smokehouse, and Mae Bertha would make sausage to put in jars or to wrap in sacks for storing. Occasionally a heifer or bull was killed and Matthew would pickle the meat in a barrel for winter. They kept a rooster that crowed at midnight and 3:00 A.M., and enough chickens to provide fourteen eggs a day. Matthew believed in feeding any animals that belonged to him, and since he couldn't afford extra for pets, the family rarely kept cats or dogs. The one pet that all the Carters remember was a puppy that appeared at cotton-picking time one year, rode around on the sacks as the children pulled them through the fields, and then disappeared at the end of the season.

ON OUR first visit to the Carters, Winifred wanted to leave before it got too dark, but Mae Bertha insisted that we wait for the school bus and meet the children. When the seven children tumbled off the bus and rushed into the living room, they stopped short at the sight of Winifred and me. When Mae Bertha explained that Jean Fairfax and the AFSC had sent us, they relaxed a little. Then Mae Bertha introduced the children as they stepped forward one by one in the small living room. Ruth, sixteen, in the eleventh grade, and Larry, fifteen, in the tenth, were in Drew High School with about two hundred white classmates. Stanley, thirteen, an eighth-grader, and Gloria, twelve, a seventh-grader, were in junior high classes located in the Drew High School building, along with more than two hundred white junior high students. Pearl, eleven, Beverly, nine, and Deborah, six, were in the fifth, third, and first grades, respectively, at the A. W. James Elementary School with almost four hundred white children. The Carter children responded shyly to our hollow-sounding question: "How are things at school?" Mostly they said, "Fine," or, "Just fine, thank you." But when Ruth spoke up about the white children who still called her names and who jumped away from her like she had "something catching," the floodgates opened. All seven children had stories to tell about the hatred directed at them in their new schools.

THE DAY I met Mae Bertha I was thirty-three years old, never married, and childless. I couldn't help wondering, "How did a woman this small, just ten years older than me, give birth to all these children?"— remembering that there were five more, grown up and living elsewhere. How did any woman raise thirteen children? How did she stand the noise, much less the pressures to feed and dress them and bear their suffering in such a small space? Where could these children find quiet places to do homework? How could they possibly meet the challenges faced daily at their new schools?

Winifred and I were very quiet as we got back in the Volkswagen to drive to the closest motel—the Downtowner in Greenville, about fifty miles away. We checked in and opened a bottle of Dewar's White Label Scotch. Already sensing the hard work ahead, we ordered steak, baked potatoes, and salad from room service. To buffer some of what we had heard from the Carter children, that night we watched TV, drank a lot, smoked a lot. And when we at last turned off the light, sleep was still far away.

In later years I loved staying at the Downtowner. Just across the street was a levee that held back the Mississippi River, and many mornings I climbed up onto it to look at the river, so wide and beautiful, even as it wielded its terrible power and shaped the lives of its Delta people.

I MET Winifred Green in May 1964 during my first trip to Mississippi. I had just been hired by the American Friends Service Committee, one of the many non-Quakers who has worked for the organization. My first assignment was to join a small group of white women in Jackson whose sensibilities had been jolted by the violence and death that followed the enrollment of the first black student at the University of Mississippi in 1962. The group, called Mississippians for Public Education, was committed to working for "peaceful school desegregation" in Jackson, Leake County, and Biloxi, the first three Mississippi school systems under court order to desegregate in the fall of 1964. The AFSC's Jean Fairfax, who was then in Mississippi working with black families to recruit their children to go to previously all-white schools, had met some of these white women, and she brought me to Mississippi to share with them AFSC's experience organizing for school desegregation.

My first day in Jackson I went to the courthouse to hear the NAACP Legal Defense and Educational Fund attorney Derrick Bell argue the Jackson school desegregation case. I happened to sit next to

Winifred, and after contemplating the huge murals on the courtroom walls—old plantation scenes replete with mammies, rollicking black children, and other supposedly happy Negroes—I leaned over to ask her how come the school board attorney had his hand on his colleague's knee. Later Winifred told me she knew right then that I was either to be avoided at all costs or befriended immediately. Luckily she chose the latter and I stayed at her house that summer. It was a hard summer for me. Many good friends were in Mississippi, engaged in the confrontational work of 1964's Freedom Summer. I was under strict orders to work *only* in the white community and *not* to be identified as a loathsome "outside agitator." Usually I was introduced as Winifred's roommate from Hollins College, down for a summer visit. One time, in Meridian, I had to hide in a closet because one of the women coming to a meeting knew I worked for the "Communist-front" AFSC. Winifred and I were able to sneak away from time to time to visit friends at Tougaloo College who were working with the Freedom Summer program. There we learned firsthand of the church burnings, house bombings, arrests, and beatings—the white citizens' response to Freedom Summer. We were at Tougaloo when the bodies of the murdered civil rights workers Michael Schwerner, James Chaney, and Andrew Goodman were finally discovered in Neshoba County, eighty miles away.

When I returned to Atlanta to the AFSC office, I wrote up a report on that first trip to the Carters' home on Busyline. Winifred and I had visited other black families in the Delta before going to the Carters and had been equally stunned by their stories. In the Issaquena-Sharkey Counties Joint School District, southwest of Sunflower County, thirty-seven families had enrolled their children in the white schools, but there, too, retribution was strong and speedy. Openly threatened, those who refused to withdraw their children within a week were either cut off from welfare, evicted from plantation homes and jobs, or fired from other employment. Thirty-three families sent their children back to the black school.

After describing these visits, the closing paragraph of my report read, "Well, on this dismal note, we left, wanting to strangle HEW, the Justice Department and all of the people who passed the Civil Rights Bill and everybody else who had allowed this kind of hope to be followed by such a wondering kind of disappointment."

The anger expressed in that report welled up from a place even deeper than the resentment raised by the trip to the Delta. Before joining the AFSC staff, I had directed a small Atlanta-based project for the United States National Student Association (USNSA) from 1960 to 1964. The association was a federation of college student governments and I had attended its national congresses each summer for four years in the 1950s when I was a student at Agnes Scott College in Decatur, Georgia. (While at college I had to get written permission from my parents to attend interracial meetings in Atlanta, because at the time segregation was the law.) Integration was one of the stated goals of the USNSA, and in 1959 it initiated a project, funded by the Field Foundation, to bring black and white college students together to discuss mutual concerns and thereby to break down the racial barriers of a new generation of Southerners. In February 1960, two months after I moved to Atlanta to set up the project, the South was suddenly forced to face its racism by student sit-ins, demonstrations, and boycotts, many of which were sponsored by the newly formed Student Non-violent Coordinating Committee (SNCC). At its first organizational meeting, SNCC chose me and Ella Baker, a longtime activist in the NAACP and later, with Dr. King, in the Southern Christian Leadership Conference (SCLC), to be advisers on its executive committee. In those early days I was the only white person on the committee.

If I am asked now about my feelings when I was young—before college, before SNCC—about growing up in Greensboro, North Carolina, about choosing to work for racial justice, the image that first comes to mind is my brown-and-yellow raincoat. I was in the fourth grade, going through the cafeteria lunch line, when Douglas, a large boy in my class, called one of the black servers a "nigger." I told him then and there that this woman was "just as good as his mother." Later that day, at play period, Douglas pushed me down in a mud puddle, and my new raincoat was all spattered. I have no idea where that brazenness came from, except that, as naive as it sounds, Sunday school lessons and the U.S. Constitution had made deep impressions, and I'd become very conscious of the gap between the values we professed and the reality of our segregated lives. All this was reinforced by fair-minded parents who let their children make their own decisions about the world around them.

Drew High School.

Two

Take Care of My Kids

On August 16, 1965, five months before I met him, Matthew Carter was wakened at 3:00 A.M. by the sound of gravel crunching. He got out of bed and went to the front window. By the time he started to ask himself, "What are all these cars doing coming in here?" gunshots were fired across the porch of his sharecropper's cabin, onto the roof and into the windows. Bullets hit a wall behind a bed where two of his children were sleeping.

No one was hurt, but Matthew moved everyone to the back room, where they stayed below window level until daylight. While he sat with his shotgun by the front door in the living room, Mae Bertha and the older children lay sleepless through the night, wondering about the path they had chosen to walk.

The Civil Rights Act of 1964 became law on July 2, 1964. Section 601 of Title VI of the act provides that

> no person in the United States shall, on the ground of race, color, or national origin, be excluded from participation in, be denied the benefit of, or be subjected to discrimination under any program or activity receiving Federal financial assistance.

This provision seemed to promise a quick and painless end to racial segregation in public schools. Instead, the Civil Rights Act marked the beginning of a further phase of white resistance. Desegregation would not become a social reality for years—more than five, in fact—across much of the South. And nowhere were segregation's death throes more prolonged and agonizing than in Sunflower County.

The United States Office of Education of the Department of Health, Education and Welfare (HEW) was instructed to enforce school desegregation throughout the nation, but there was general confusion about just *how* to do it. HEW told school systems to develop desegregation plans but offered unclear guidelines for compliance. In Mississippi, particularly in poor rural areas, school officials were well aware that they couldn't operate their schools without federal funds, but because many of their board members believed that integration would effectively destroy public education in their districts, superintendents and principals devised so-called freedom of choice plans that capitalized on HEW's confusion. These plans ostensibly gave all parents the right to send their children to the schools of their choice.

By the time Mississippi began implementing freedom of choice plans, similar policies had already been court-sanctioned in several school districts in other states, including New Orleans and Baton Rouge in Louisiana. In 1965, HEW approved hundreds of such plans throughout the South, hoping that they would produce at least a modicum of integration in rural areas. Mississippi's freedom of choice policy, however, seemed consciously conceived as a means of preventing black children from attending white schools in significant numbers. Moreover, integration based on such a policy would be a one-way street—the school boards knew no white children would apply to attend black schools. It took HEW a while to catch on.

Lloyd Henderson, the HEW staff member assigned to Mississippi in 1965, wrote ten years later in the *Journal of Law and Education:*

> Personally, I am convinced that Federal officials genuinely
> believed that the schools would be desegregated in fact if children
> were given the opportunity to choose . . . and that if the plans
> were administered honestly, black children would enroll in the
> white schools in droves, thus causing white children to be
> assigned to the black schools.

Henderson wondered how federal officials could have expected southern black families to dare to send their children to all-white schools after more than a century of racism and violence: "It seems incredible now that anyone could seriously have believed that an economically dependent class of people could assume the burden of bringing about compliance with the federal law. Under such circumstances choice could never be free."

Although their house on the Pemble Plantation was nine miles from Drew, the Carter children were included in the freedom of choice plan for the Drew Municipal Separate School District. The five white men who constituted the school district's board of trustees knew that failure to obey the federal law would mean the loss of a quarter of a million dollars. Because the Drew public school system could not operate without that money, the board worked to create a plan that would be acceptable to HEW but that would guarantee the least possible school desegregation.

Early in May of 1965, black children brought notices home from school that their parents were to sign and return if they wanted their children to attend school straight through from September to May. If they did not sign, their children would continue to attend split sessions. The notices did not indicate that the choice of the nine-month session was linked to school desegregation.

Mae Bertha read the notice and told her children, "I'm going to sign these papers so you can start to school in September." At the end of May, the Carter children reported to their parents that they were the only ones to sign the papers. According to the children, all the other parents said their children had to pick cotton. In fact, Mae Bertha was herself uncertain how the family would survive if the children did indeed attend school for nine consecutive months.

The Carters heard nothing more from the school system until, on July 12, the Drew school board unanimously adopted a resolution outlining the school desegregation plan accepted by HEW. The federal guidelines mandated that the plan be published in the local papers and that all parents and guardians be given adequate notice. The full text of the school board resolution appeared in the *Sunflower County News* on Thursday, August 5, 1965. It began:

WHEREAS, as the result of judicial decisions and
statutes enacted by the Congress of the United
States, it is without question that enforced
racial segregation in the public schools of
Mississippi and other States is illegal,
and that compulsory separate but equal
school systems for the white and negro races
will be no longer permitted . . .

The rest of the resolution outlined the Drew plan in detail. Parents or guardians of all pupils, white and black, were to exercise their choice by returning a registration form to any of the five schools in the district. The school registration period was from August 9 to August 13. The Drew school system was so certain of its control of the situation that it opened all twelve grades to freedom of choice, rather than the minimum of three required by HEW.

August came, and Drew, like dozens of other Delta towns, waited. In 1965, Main Street in Drew was only a few blocks long, and all its one-story businesses were on the west side of the street. Diagonal parking places were marked on the curb in front of Timberlake's Pharmacy, Fred's Five and Dime, two office fronts, Western Auto, and Miller's Furniture. The other side of the street fronted the tracks where the trains came to pick up cotton at the gins north and south of town. Drew's few residential streets, segregated by race, began at Main and, like Main Street itself, ended in cotton fields that circled the town. Seemingly unchanged by any Washington directives, or by the tumult of Freedom Summer the previous year, Drew dozed under the August blanket of heat and humidity.

Although Drew was only nine miles from the Carters' house, the family had always done most of its shopping, visiting, and church-going in Merigold and Cleveland. They knew little of Drew's long-standing reputation as a violent town. The violence was aimed at everyone, but particularly at blacks. When he was young, Matthew had heard black men on the plantations talk about a sort of red-light district in Drew in the 1930s called Crocker's Cypress Canebrake. The area belonged to a Mr. Crocker, a white man who had built shotgun houses to offer accommodations and entertainment to the black workers who hired themselves out to pick cotton in the surrounding fields. At the Canebrake, a man could play cards, listen to music on the Victrola, find prostitutes, and dance and drink. Crocker allowed only blacks into the Canebrake and sat with a shotgun each night guarding the entrance against raids from the local police.

What the Carters did not know was that in more recent years Drew had become "wide open" to whites from miles around who came to take advantage of the town's unrestricted gambling and prostitution. Nor had they heard of the Sunday morning game of "blood trails" played by young blacks on their way to church in Drew. The game involved finding a trail of blood left on the street from Saturday night and making bets whether it was white blood (which would lead to the doctor's house) or black blood (which would lead off into the woods).

For years, law enforcement in Drew had seemed to be dictated by the proximity of Parchman State Penitentiary, seven miles away. The fear of escaped convicts, an occurrence more imagined than real, gave law officers an easy excuse for searches, arrests, and shootings. Dewey Roth was marshal in Drew from 1933 to 1943. Widely known as cruel and violent, he had served a term in prison for shooting another man, but was appointed marshal upon his release. He became known for using his gun to enforce the law and for shooting blacks on the streets of Drew. Finally he went too far, even by Mississippi standards: in 1946, he shot Robert Prentis Moody, a young white man from Drew. Moody, who had gotten out of the navy just two weeks earlier, had met some old buddies and they were standing and talking on South Main Street in downtown Drew. Roth, who had been drinking, came up to the group and told them he was tired of service men coming home and trying to run *his* town. Moody answered that the group was just talking. Roth said, "Shut up, you little black-haired son of a bitch." Moody hit Roth, and Roth pulled out his gun and shot and killed Moody on the spot. Roth was sent back to Parchman, where he died in 1955. By 1965 Drew had quieted down some, but the undercurrent of racial violence remained. The white population believed in preserving the racial status quo at all costs. The black population lived in subservience and fear.

Although Mae Bertha may not have known all about Drew's past, she understood the politics of race. Not long after we met, she told me, "You have to live in Mississippi to really know about Mississippi. The white folk think they know black people and the black people think they know white people. Now the black people know what the white man likes before he tells them and some things he don't even have to be told. White man didn't even have to go to the black's house and say, 'Don't send your child to the school,' 'cause we know what the white man likes. So we know one another. And they were sure that they had fixed everything around Drew so no blacks would be coming around their schools. They were so sure of that. But they didn't know about us out there on the farm."

On August 6, the Drew school district mailed freedom of choice notices to all parents of school-age children. Mae Bertha was away visiting relatives in St. Louis when the notice arrived at the farm. She had left Matthew in charge, along with Ruth, who was about to enter the eleventh grade and was the oldest Carter child still at home. Ruth opened the letter from the school district, read it, and made up her mind immediately. She wanted to go to the white school. She wanted to get away from the cotton fields. Underlying these immediate desires, Ruth also believed that her family's choice might eventually change the social order, which she had hated since she was a little girl. When she was only nine years old, she had begged her parents with such intensity to let her live for a year with her grandmother in Toledo, Ohio, that they had allowed her to go.

The letter Ruth read said that students age fourteen and older were permitted to sign their own choice forms. Larry and Stanley, who would enter the white high school with Ruth, also sensed what this decision could mean. The three high-schoolers discussed going to the white schools with the four younger school-age children. By supper time, all seven had convinced each other it was the right thing to do.

Ruth immediately wrote a letter to her mother in St. Louis: "Come home. You have some papers to sign saying what school we want to go to. We want to go to the all-white school." The day Mae Bertha received the letter, her cousin drove her back to Drew. She came home to hear all seven of the children tell her that yes, indeed, they wanted to go to the all-white school. Matthew and Mae Bertha answered their children, "If you want to go, we want you to go."

IT WAS already ninety degrees at seven in the morning on August 12 when Mae Bertha and Matthew climbed into their ancient green pickup truck. Mae Bertha wore a cotton print dress and Matthew had on khaki pants and a short-sleeved blue shirt. The enormity of what they were about to do threatened to overwhelm them both. In silence, they drove the nine miles into Drew to deliver the freedom of choice papers. Just inside the town limits, Mae Bertha finally blurted out, "Matthew, I feel like everyone knows where we're going."

When they stopped the truck in front of Drew High School, everything was quiet. It was still more than two weeks before the first day of school and no one was outside the building. Inside, Mae Bertha and Matthew looked around. It looked shiny and well kept in comparison with all-black Hunter High School. A secretary showed them into the principal's office. There they handed the papers to the principal, C. M. Reid. Mae Bertha remembered how he "got red all over" but said not a word. Mae Bertha and Matthew stood awkwardly in front of his desk for a few moments before they turned and left. They had no way of knowing that not only were they the only black parents to desegregate the Drew system, they were the only ones in all of Sunflower County.

WHEN MAE Bertha's five oldest children had started school in the late 1940s, the educational system for blacks lagged far behind its white counterpart. A 1937 study of Mississippi's educational system commissioned by the Peabody Fund found 105 schools for black children in Sunflower County, almost all of them located in dilapidated one-room church buildings or in old plantation buildings donated by the landowner—who also often hired the teacher and provided wood for the stove in winter. There was not a single black high school in the county. The report recommended that 81 of the "deplorable" schools be abandoned and new ones built. Virtually none of the Peabody Fund's recommendations were followed.

Years later, when Mae Bertha and I visited Isabel Lee in Indianola, twenty-seven miles from Drew, we heard the most amazing stories about attempts by the Anna T. Jeanes Program to improve the early educational system for black children in Sunflower County and throughout the South. The Jeanes program began in 1908 when the Quaker philanthropist Anna T. Jeanes contributed one million dollars to set up the Negro Rural School Fund to serve the "masses of the people at the bottom, little people, forgotten, in out-of-the-way places." In cooperation with state and county school systems in fourteen southern states, the program she established gave funds to improve buildings, buy equipment and books, and hire supervisors to check on the continuing needs and quality of the black schools. Isabel Lee's sister, Lillian Rogers Johnson, had been the first Jeanes supervisor for black public schools in Sunflower County, serving from 1928 to 1943. White school officials had mixed feelings about the Jeanes program. They were glad for the money to hire teachers and improve buildings, because it meant that more of the government school funds could be channeled to the all-white schools. At the same time, however, some of the Jeanes supervisors, in their advocacy for better educational opportunities for blacks, were openly critical of and antagonistic toward white school officials.

By the early 1930s, Mississippi had Jeanes supervisors in twenty-six counties, including Sunflower. Mrs. Lee showed Mae Bertha and me old photographs of some of the 134 schools in Sunflower County for which Lillian Rogers Johnson had responsibility. "My sister," Mrs.

Lee told us, "was heartsick at the terrible conditions in most of those schools. But what made her the saddest was the teachers. Lillian said that sometimes the school superintendent would hire, as teachers, cooks from surrounding plantations who could barely read and write themselves. Lillian would arrive at these schools to find the children singing or even taking rest time and sleeping at their desks; the teachers knew that if Lillian were to rate their abilities as teachers, they would fail. She also told us that black principals would demand money from the teachers they helped to pass the exams given at the end of summer school programs set up specifically to upgrade the skills of black teachers. Some of the black principals actually extorted part of the black teachers' salaries in exchange for a promise to hire them again the following year. Lillian would report these injustices, and many principals, white and black, in Sunflower County, considered her their 'mortal enemy.'"

Over the years, the state had developed a formula for funding the educational system that was based on the total number of school-children, regardless of color, but the lion's share of the allotted funds continued to go to the white schools. Inequities in the two systems were openly justified by some planters who saw educational opportunities for blacks as paving the way for an exodus from their cotton fields, much as Mae Bertha's own older children had fled. Others considered education for blacks a waste of money, believing that no matter the amount of education, "a million years from now, a nigger will still be a nigger in the South."

In 1950, a group of forty-nine white people concerned about education for blacks in Sunflower County met and appointed an interracial committee to investigate a survey of schools made by the Department of Education at the University of Mississippi. The survey's findings confirmed their fears: most of the county schools for blacks ended at the tenth grade, and of the twenty thousand black children in the county between the ages of six and twenty-one, only half were enrolled in school. Almost none of the teachers in black schools had a college education, only a third had completed high school, and five had progressed only to the ninth grade. Only two school buses served more than one hundred black schools; most black children had to walk to school.

With the NAACP challenging the principle of segregation in the courts, the Sunflower County school board was pressured to make some effort to improve black schools. Hunter High School for blacks was built in 1955, and officials pointed out that it was the same color brick as the white high school. By the 1960s, however, steadily increasing disparities in per pupil expenditures; in education levels of teachers; and in physical plants, curricula, and transportation exposed the truth about a system that still blatantly discriminated against African-Americans.

Mae Bertha and Matthew had gone through such a system themselves and had then watched their first five children endure many of the same inequities. Now they had a chance to change circumstances for the rest of their children, and the "choice" was clear. When I asked her about their decision, that first day in the sharecropper house on Busyline, Mae Bertha's voice rose in a response almost like an oration: "Why I decided that I wanted them to go was I was tired of my kids coming home with pages torn out of worn-out books that come from the white school. I was tired of them riding on these old raggedy buses after the white children didn't want to ride on them anymore. I was just tired, and I thought if they go to this all-white school they will get a better education there. Plus the school board is all white and over both the white and black schools, but that school board was more concerned about their kids than they were about black kids— always have been.

"In fact, when you would go to the black school, the kids were eating lunch once or maybe twice a week. The teacher would get just so many tickets to issue out, and I would hear my kids say something like, 'Well maybe I'll get a ticket today to eat,' and then sometimes they'd come home and say, 'Well I was lucky today. I got a ticket to eat.' And see, them white children was eating lunch every day. So that's why we signed the papers. We had seven children to go, three to the elementary school and four to the high school. So we integrated both of those schools."

News of the enrollment of the Carter children spread like wildfire through Sunflower County, and Mae Bertha felt sure that someone from the school superintendent's office had called Mr. Thornton, the plantation overseer. Early the next morning, Thornton drove up in his pickup truck and blew his horn in front of the Carters' house.

"Mary," Matthew said softly over his shoulder, using his special name for Mae Bertha, "it's starting." He went outside to the waiting truck.

Thornton's mission was simple. He told Matthew that he'd heard about the enrollment and he believed that the best thing for Matthew and Mae Bertha would be to go back to Drew and withdraw the children. He believed they could get a better education at the black school. He explained to Matthew that the children would have no friends at the white school. Neither black folks nor white folks would have anything to do with the Carters anymore. Those poor whites who lived over on federal land near the Carters would cause them a lot of trouble. He offered to go to Drew with Matthew and help "withdraw 'em out." Matthew said that he didn't need the help and that if he decided to withdraw the children, he would go himself.

Mae Bertha, who had been standing on the porch listening, went into the house. She came out a few minutes later carrying a chair, a single record, and a little record player. She set the player carefully on the chair, close to the porch door so the cord could reach an outlet in the living room, and she put on the record. It was the June 11, 1963, speech that President Kennedy had given on national radio and television calling for the Civil Rights Act. The speech was delivered only a few hours before the Mississippi NAACP leader Medgar Evers was murdered outside his Jackson home just after midnight on June 12. Mae Bertha's son Man had sent her the record, and it was one of her greatest treasures. Mae Bertha started the record player and turned the volume way up:

> And when Americans are sent to Vietnam or West Berlin, we do not ask for whites only. It ought to be possible, therefore, for American students of any color to attend any public institution they select without having to be backed up by troops. . . . We are confronted primarily with a moral issue. It is as old as the Scriptures and as clear as the American Constitution.

I can imagine Mae Bertha standing by her front door, firm and proud, arms folded, as John Kennedy's voice spilled across the early morning silence—talking about what it was like to be a black person in America, and about the great opportunities available to all except to black children. Mae Bertha let the record play on and on as Matthew stood out by the truck. Finally Thornton said he would go down to the barn to give Matthew time to talk to Mae Bertha.

Mae Bertha remembered what she had then said to Matthew. "You go out there, to the barn," she had told him, "and you tell Mr. Thornton that I am a grown woman. I birthed those children and bore the pain. He cannot tell me what to do about my children, like withdrawing my children out. And I'd be a fool to try and tell him where to send his kids."

Matthew answered, "Well, Mary, I'm not going to tell him all that." They told Thornton simply that they had decided to keep their children in the white school.

The morning after the shots were fired into the house, a neighbor took Mae Bertha to Cleveland, Mississippi, to see Amzie Moore, a black businessman and NAACP leader, and Charles McLaurin, the Sunflower County project director for the Student Nonviolent Coordinating Committee. When Mae Bertha finished telling her story, Moore and McLaurin called the FBI in Jackson. The next day Deputy Sheriff John Sidney Parker received a call at his home from the county sheriff's office in Indianola, five miles away. Parker was asked to go to Drew to join an FBI agent to investigate the shooting at the Carters'. The agent was from FBI Headquarters in Washington; he had flown in because local FBI agents were on other assignments. He and Parker drove in separate cars to Busyline. When they reached the Carters' house, the agent's first question to Mae Bertha was, why had she gone all the way to Cleveland to call when she could have gone to some of the white people's houses nearby?

Mae Bertha chuckled at the memory of her response. "Go where?"

she answered the agent. "Let me tell you one thing, man, I ain't got confidence in any white man living in Mississippi. I can't be going to no white folks' house calling, 'cause that's probably the ones who shot into my house."

Parker and the FBI agent inspected the Carters' house carefully. Mr. Thornton, the plantation overseer, was present as well and helped them take each of the bullets out of the walls. The Washington agent took the bullets with him as evidence, and that was the last the Carters heard from the FBI or anyone else about the shooting. The story circulated in the white community was that the Carters, prompted by black militants eager for publicity, had done the shooting themselves.

News of the shooting spread as quickly in the black community as news of the Carters' enrollment had spread in the white. Amzie Moore sent Charles McLaurin to the Carters with fifty dollars for food. "Amzie told me how to get there," McLaurin recalled, "and I went on. But I will tell you the truth, I was frightened. I couldn't figure the Carters out, and I just had to see these people. That morning I drove out to what we called 'plumnelly' to see these people living on this white man's place, knowing they had gone to downtown Drew, fixing to put these children in the white school. It frightened me. I figured they were going to be killed. I believe I made three or four trips out there and was scared every time. I thought about how we had already had Schwerner, Chaney, and Goodman murdered by these patroling Klansmen, and every trip I thought that one might be right around the corner somewhere. And I was supposed to be the brave one, you know."

As the first day of school drew near, life for the Carters proceeded as usual, for the most part. The older children picked cotton, but they talked among themselves about the changes that would soon take place. Matthew had extra work in the evenings sewing underwear for the girls from cotton sacks and hemming dresses. The children remember the day he announced, "Mary, I have stopped smoking. We need money too much to send these children."

FAR AWAY, in Philadelphia, the American Friends Service Committee was trying to get a firsthand report on school desegregation in the Delta to pass on to appropriate federal agencies. Jean Fairfax, the director of southern programs for AFSC, had asked Prathia Hall Wynn, an SNCC field secretary, to monitor compliance in the Sunflower County area. Charles McLaurin had told Wynn about the shooting incident at the Carters' and she wanted to visit them, but her coworkers in Sunflower advised her of the difficulties they had faced in the county and warned her not to go into Drew unless she was willing to risk arrest.

In the middle of August 1965, Wynn reported to Jean Fairfax that several families on Sunflower County plantations had considered turning in the freedom of choice forms. "A Mr. Jones who lives on a plantation near the Carter family came into Ruleville to talk to me. He talked about the fear that kept people from transferring their children. He said that many families discussed the matter when the forms were first sent out. They were afraid of reprisals. The shooting incident had ruled out the choice completely."

Alarmed by Wynn's report, Fairfax called John Doar, assistant attorney general in the U.S. Justice Department's Civil Rights Division. Doar wrote a memo to the director of the Federal Bureau of Investigation in which he outlined the Drew situation and suggested that the FBI "confirm the date of school opening. Observe each of the desegregating schools on the day that the Negro pupils first enter. Report immediately any interference or threatened interference with the attendance of the children. Any build-up of crowds in the area of a desegregating school should be immediately reported."

The only money the Carters had in August 1965 was forty dollars hidden in a mattress, saved in case Mae Bertha needed to go to Toledo to see her mother, Luvenia. Matthew knew that Mae Bertha missed Luvenia and he had insisted that they save the bus fare. The share-cropping system of buying food and supplies on credit from the plantation store, paying when there was a little money, and always being beholden to the plantation owner and in debt to his store was still very much in effect at Pemble Plantation. A few days after enrolling his children in the white schools, Matthew Carter went to Bob's, the store that usually gave him credit. Had he heard right? the owner asked. Had Matthew been over to Drew and enrolled his kids in the all-white school? When Matthew nodded, he was told he had until three o'clock that day to take the children out of the school. Matthew went home with only a little package of food in his hands, rather than the weekly order of staples needed to feed ten people. Mae Bertha took the forty-dollar bus fare from under the mattress and gave it to Matthew, who drove to Cleveland to buy food.

For several days it seemed that the enrollment of the children and the night shooting had never occurred. No one came to the house. But the bullet holes had made the truth clear for the Carters. The family slept on the floor for three nights after the shooting.

Mae Bertha told me what she thought about during those tense days; she remembered what a preacher in Cleveland had said once: "Everybody's afraid and it's okay to be afraid but you can't let it stop you." She explained to me that the "covering" she had felt first as a young girl came over her during those days and she felt confident that her family was protected. On the fourth night after the shooting the family moved off the floor and back into its beds and never slept on the floor again. Mae Bertha told Matthew that she was calling to the Lord.

Meanwhile, the rest of the SNCC workers in Ruleville and Cleveland spread the word that the Carters were in danger and needed help. Amzie Moore had contacted the Delta Ministry in Greenville. Its representative, Reverend Owen Brooks, came to visit the Carters and brought money for food. The Delta Ministry had been established by the National Council of Churches to be its "presence" during the tumultuous Freedom Summer activities of 1964, and it continues to operate to this day. With a main office in Greenville and full-time staff in several towns outside the Delta, the ministry worked not only with local leaders in community development programs but also to help people like the Carters.

Several days after the shooting, Mae Bertha was visiting one of her good friends down the road, "trying to feel better," when Beverly came running over and told her mother that a white lady and a black lady had come to talk to her. The two women were from New York and were part of a group investigating the needs of families like the Carters. Mae Bertha told them about the shooting and the women took pictures of the bullet holes. They took notes as Mae Bertha described the family's needs—food, lunch money for the children, clothing. After a second visit the following day, the two women promised to go back to New York to tell the story to churches, lodges, and other groups that would send money to the Carters.

Mae Bertha has forgotten none of the details of September 3, 1965, the first day of school in Drew, Mississippi. Matthew was up at 5:30 A.M. to get water from the pump, heat up the kettle and the big dishpan on the stove, and fill the tub in the bedroom. He bathed and dressed Deborah and Beverly, the two youngest girls. The older ones got themselves ready. Mae Bertha remembers how mute they were. She also remembers how she lay in bed wondering if she had the strength and will to get up and face the fear that pressed in upon her. It was the first day in Drew history that black children would attend public school with white children. Those black children were hers. They would be desegregating both Drew High School and A. W. James Elementary School. But the principles of "freedom of choice" and "desegregation" seemed high-flown and irrelevant as Mae Bertha imagined the day that stretched ahead of Deborah, Beverly, Pearl, Gloria, Stanley, Larry, and Ruth.

After breakfast, the children, each with a quarter for lunch, went out on the porch with Mae Bertha to wait for the school bus. By 7:30 the sun was out in strength. The heavy wet heat of late summer settled over the cotton fields. Would the new bus driver know where to stop for the Carters? Would they be the first ones on the bus? Where would they sit? How would they know where to go when they got to school?

A newly painted yellow school bus was spotted turning onto Busyline. In silence Mae Bertha and the children watched its slow passage down the rutted dirt road. Finally the bus stopped at the house and the children stepped down from the porch and one by one climbed in to discover that they were indeed the first to be picked up. They sat two by two near the front of the bus, with Ruth taking a seat by herself.

Mae Bertha stayed on the porch and watched until the bus was out of sight. Her eyes filled and she took the baby, Carl, back into the house. She later wrote Jean Fairfax:

When the bus pulled off, I went in and fell down cross the bed and prayed. I stayed on that bed and didn't do no work that day. No "covering" in sight this time. I didn't feel good and stayed cross the bed and when I heard the bus coming, I went back to the porch. When they came off one by one, then I was released until the next morning. But the next morning I felt the same way, depressed, nervous, praying to God. I wasn't saying a whole lot of words; just saying, "take care of my kids"—no time for all those other words. And I didn't do housecleaning until the children came home. After about a month, I started easing up a little bit. I had prayed to God so much! I had been going to church and talking about trusting in Jesus, but I never trusted Jesus until my children went to that all-white school. That school for sure brought me to God!

Where Emmett Till was rumored to have been murdered in 1955—the deserted barn as it appears today on the outskirts of Drew.

Three

Advancement for Colored People

On a Sunday afternoon in July 1955, ten years before the Carters signed the freedom of choice papers, Reverend Anderson arrived at their house in a battered bus. The young minister, a Christian Scientist, had himself recently begun sharecropping at the nearby Zumbro Plantation. Anderson visited neighboring sharecroppers' homes often, sometimes bringing along his twin daughters, Mary and Martha, and he was a well-known figure in the Delta. What was not generally known, though, was the purpose of his visits. Reverend J. J. O. Anderson was the treasurer and membership recruiter for the small NAACP chapter in nearby Cleveland, Mississippi. He was "writing up" for the NAACP.

That July Sunday, Reverend Anderson sat on the porch with Mae
Bertha and Matthew and began to tell them of this group that was
working for the rights of colored people. Mae Bertha asked, "What does
NAACP mean?" As he described the organization, she heard only four
words: "Well, then, if it's *advancement for colored people*, I want to join!"

He said, "That's what it does." She and Matthew and the four
oldest children paid their dollar each and joined the NAACP.

In the early 1950s, when the NAACP was suing to challenge segregated and inferior educational systems for black children, even mentioning the organization's acronym evoked venom and hatred in most
white Mississippians. Since the early days of slavery, educated blacks
had represented a threat to the segregated system, and the proponents
of that system were prepared to prevent equal education and integration, whatever the cost.

In August 1950, Thurgood Marshall, then head of the NAACP
Legal Defense and Educational Fund in New York City, wrote a memo
to Gloster Current, the NAACP branch director, also in New York,
about the difficulty in getting the right person to lead the Mississippi
branch:

> I think before we criticize . . . people in Mississippi, we had better
> first consider Mississippi. I have been there several times and I
> have worked on many matters in Mississippi and it is the worst
> hole in the world. The only way to do a good job in Mississippi is
> to have someone there who knows Mississippi and who knows
> the people. There are places in Mississippi where they will not
> even talk to anyone, white or colored, who is from outside the
> state. . . . As for building up young people in the Association, I, of

course, agree with this. However, it has been my experience that all young people run out of Mississippi as fast as they can and this goes for white and Negro.

Despite the danger, in 1951 black leaders in Cleveland, Mississippi, organized an NAACP branch and elected Amzie Moore, a young businessman, its president. Moore had served in a segregated army unit in the South Pacific until 1946, which had reinforced his awareness of the contradiction inherent in fighting for a country that separated black soldiers from white soldiers. He came out of the army determined to start his own business in Cleveland and to establish some independence from the vagaries of discrimination and segregation. He built a store and filling station on Highway 61, the main highway through Cleveland. He worked for the U.S. Post Office, too, and even though he was brash and outspoken, his federal job insulated him somewhat from local white economic pressure.

A few years later, in 1958, Amzie Moore received a grant of $586 from the American Friends Service Committee to help him make monthly payments on the filling station and to buy some auto equipment. The committee's recommendation for funding noted that "there is a reasonable chance for Amzie Moore to remain in Cleveland and serve as a leader in the community." It was money well spent. As a secure businessman, Moore could help bring civil rights workers to Mississippi in the 1960s and could aid people like the Carters as they fought for their rights.

When I visit Mae Bertha today, if I don't want to drive all the way to Greenville, I usually stay at the Cleveland Inn, which is just across the road from Moore's filling station, now unpainted and in disrepair.

In 1991, Mae Bertha took me to see Moore's widow, who gave me an old postcard of the filling station. The card shows a neat white structure called the Pan-Am Cafe. Red stripes on the sign emphasize the name, painted in blue. Red gas pumps and soda machines are in front of the building. The back of the postcard reads:

MOORE'S ENTERPRISES

Completed July 1954 at the cost of approximately $35,000.00
"We're interested in your complete satisfaction"
Ultra-modern Service Station—Cafe—Beauty Salon
Air Conditioned throughout.
Quality Auto Service 24 hours a day

MR. AND MRS. AMZIE MOORE, OWNERS-MANAGERS

Mrs. Moore told us the one thing her husband made clear before he died in 1980 was that she "must not sell the filling station because it was so hard to get and so hard to keep."

It was Amzie Moore who helped organize Reverend Anderson's travels during the 1950s from plantation to plantation in the Delta, quietly signing up people for the NAACP. Soon small groups of new members were slipping away in the evening to go to NAACP activities together. Mae Bertha loved going to the meetings at New Kingdom Baptist Church in Cleveland every Wednesday night and she and Matthew encouraged trusted friends and neighbors to come along with them. "It broadens my concepts," she told her friends. "Someone might bring a newspaper and tell us what's happening somewhere else. And that listening to other people make speeches, that helps me along the way." The older children often joined Mae

Bertha, and she and Matthew always brought the youngest ones in their arms.

But it was dangerous business. There were informers on most plantations waiting to pass on information about meeting places and meeting times and the names of those going. Once, when Mae Bertha discovered a "leak" in her community, she devised a strategy to plug it. The Cleveland branch had an opportunity in 1956 to travel by bus to Jackson to hear Roy Wilkins, the NAACP's national executive secretary. The Delta members were excited and afraid, and Mae Bertha, thinking of the informer, told Matthew, "I'll tell you what we'll do—we'll get his wife to go along, and then he won't be telling on us." After that trip, she made sure that the informer's wife was involved in all their activities.

The U.S. Supreme Court decision on May 17, 1954, in *Brown v. Board of Education*, which declared that segregated public schools were unconstitutional, signaled a closing of the ranks among white Mississippi segregationists. For example, Tom Brady, a Yale-educated circuit court judge from Brookhaven, issued a pamphlet that called the day of the decision "Black Monday"; in it he railed against communism and predicted that integration would lead to the "amalgamation" of the races.

In Indianola, Sunflower's county seat, the Citizens' Council was organized for the purpose of preserving segregation, and councils quickly sprang up across the state to recruit politicians, businessmen, and other respected pillars of the white community. United States Senator James Eastland, the owner of a 5,800-acre cotton plantation near Doddsville, in Sunflower County, called for "a great crusade . . . to fight the CIO [Congress of Industrial Organizations], the NAACP . . . the conscienceless pressure groups who are attempting our destruction" through "the illegal, immoral and sinful doctrine of school desegregation."

Mae Bertha first learned of the Supreme Court decision from a friend at church who said to her, "You know, the Supreme Court handed down something on the desegregation of public schools."

Mae Bertha told me it was the first time she had ever heard the word *desegregation*.

"You're gonna have to break that down for me," she said to her friend. "What's desegregation?"

"It's integration."

"What's integration?"

"Well, what they're saying—they're talking about black and white children will all be going to school together."

"Well, I'll be glad, because when that day come our children won't be starting to school in November, and stopping all the time to pick cotton. I know they will start in September and go nine months like the white children." But for Mae Bertha Carter it would be eleven years and many heartbreaks later before such a welcome change would happen for her family.

In spite of the gathering opposition, the NAACP continued to press ahead. In December 1954, Medgar Evers, himself a native of Mississippi, was selected as the state's first NAACP field secretary. Evers was born in Decatur, Mississippi, in 1926. Like Amzie Moore, he had served in the army during World War II. He had worked in Chicago and traveled to other states, but he loved Mississippi and had returned with the belief that its flaws could be corrected. Based in Jackson and traveling extensively, Evers encouraged NAACP membership drives and branch organization in every community in which any black leadership had emerged. By December 1955 there were thirty-eight branches in the state and a membership of 4,026, an increase of about 1,000 people. In his annual report to the national office in 1955, Evers described the economic pressures suffered by blacks involved with the NAACP—inequitable cotton allotments, job loss, evictions—as well as the direct threats of violence against them. He described how members would ask to be removed from the NAACP mailing list because the post office had spread word of their membership and they were afraid of the consequences. But Evers did not despair. In that same report he wrote, "Even in the state of Mississippi where it is akin to a crime to be a member, Negroes gloat at being a member of the one non-compromising organization that is championing the cause of the Negro for first-class citizenship."

One of the worst lynchings in Mississippi history—one that evoked horror and outrage around the world—happened during Evers's first year on the job as field secretary. Emmett Till, a fourteen-year-old black youth from Chicago, Illinois, was visiting his relatives in Leflore County, which borders Sunflower. He was said to have whistled at the wife of one of the men later accused of the lynching, Roy Bryant. Bryant and his half brother J. W. Milam were alleged to have kidnapped Emmett Till in the middle of the night and then beat him to death. Till's killers weighted his body with a one-hundred-pound cotton-gin fan and threw it into the Tallahatchie River. In a hurried trial, a Leflore County grand jury failed to bring an indictment because Bryant's defense maintained that the body taken from the river was not Emmett Till's, despite identification of the body by Mamie Bradley, Till's mother, and the fact that Till's ring was recovered on the body. Bryant's lawyer told the jury that there were people in the United

States who would not hesitate to put a "rotten stinking body in the river in the hope he would be identified as Emmett Till." Mrs. Bradley took her son's body back to Chicago, where it lay in state for three days while more than 600,000 people passed in an unending procession. Mrs. Bradley allowed *Jet* magazine to publish a photo of the brutally battered body, and the international press reported the story in all its tragic detail. The journalist William Bradford Huie interviewed Bryant and Milam several months after their acquittal. In exchange for cash, they admitted to him that they had murdered Emmett Till.

The horror of the murder and the injustice of the acquittal engendered confusion and conflict in the Delta's black community. Many blacks were terror-stricken. Stories and rumors spread. One was that the murder took place in a barn on the road to Hitchin' Hill, very near the Carters' house in Sunflower County. The barn was owned by some relatives of the alleged killers. Willie Reed, a nineteen-year-old black man, said that he heard screams and the sounds of a beating coming from the barn that night when he was fetching water, and that he saw men bring a body out and put it in a truck. Medgar Evers and a team of other NAACP officials, working to identify witnesses for the prosecution, located Willie Reed, and he testified at the trial. Soon after the case was dismissed, Medgar Evers bought Reed some new clothes and put him and another witness, Alonzo Bradley, on a train to Chicago. Other blacks who lived near the barn or had passed it that night quickly and quietly moved away.

Five miles from Hitchin' Hill, Naomi Carter, just turned thirteen herself at the time, finally admitted to her parents that whenever it got dark and her parents weren't home, she and the younger children always hid inside the house. For Naomi and countless other black children, the Till murder instilled fear, but it also made them loathe racism. By the 1960s, many of these young people were working to launch freedom schools and voter registration drives, which would finally change Mississippi once and for all.

Despite the Till murder—or maybe in response to it—the Cleveland NAACP branch grew to be one of the strongest in the rural South: in January 1956 it reported that the 1955 membership drive had recruited 397 people, bringing total membership to 475 paid adults and 30 youths. The Carters continued to attend the Wednesday meetings and listened to stories of people like Rosa Parks, who had sparked the Montgomery, Alabama, bus boycott when she sat in the white section of a city bus in 1956. They heard about a young preacher named Martin Luther King, Jr., whose stirring words and daring actions were inspiring black people across the South. Mae Bertha recalled how, in 1960, the group marveled at the newspaper account of four black students who had dared to sit at a lunch counter at a Woolworth's in Greensboro, North Carolina. "Ain't none of that ever gonna happen in Mississippi or get to us out here on these plantations," Mae Bertha remembered telling Matthew and the children.

Despite their doubts about social change ever reaching Drew, Mae Bertha and Matthew stayed constant in their own efforts to educate their children. In 1957, their oldest child, Edna, boarded a bus for Nashville, Tennessee. "When Edna was born in 1939," Mae Bertha said to me, "I told that beautiful little girl that she would never grow up and be working all her days in a cotton field." And indeed Edna spent most of her childhood with her grandmother Maggie Griffin while Mae Bertha worked in the fields. As Edna grew up, Maggie encouraged her to become a teacher and saved money to send her to college.

Maggie sold insurance, kept the church accounts, and sold candy to church members and neighbors. The family joked that she'd "hold on to a silver dollar so hard, the eagle would holler." By the time Edna graduated from high school—at the age of seventeen—Maggie had saved three hundred dollars, a significant sum in those days. Edna told her grandmother she really didn't want to be a teacher, but she did want to go to the National School of Business in Nashville, which taught typing, shorthand, and accounting. When she left on the bus for Nashville, Edna Carter had never used a telephone.

The next four oldest children after Edna also left home as soon as they graduated from Hunter High School: Bertha went to Toledo to live with her uncle; Naomi went to Nashville to stay with Edna; Man and J.C. both joined the air force. Matthew and Mae Bertha and their eight other children moved to Busyline; they chose not to join the tide leaving the Delta, drawn by dreams of employment in the North. Mae Bertha wrote to her mother in Toledo, "Mama, my family is never really hungry"; and when the rest of the family in Ohio urged Mae Bertha to move there, she replied, "It's dark up there, you be getting up at daybreak to ride on a cold bus to a gray factory with a bunch of strangers and ain't no room for a vegetable garden or a chicken."

Mae Bertha did get discouraged and told me of feeling trapped sometimes: "We just had to work so hard all the time, and when we weren't making our own crops we had to do day labor just to make ends meet." The Carters often picked on the neighboring Sunflower Plantation, land parceled out in 1937 by the U.S. Rural Rehabilitation Administration under the Sunflower Resettlement Program. As part of the program, white farmers, most of whom came from Mississippi hill country, could rent forty acres of land with a house and a barn in Sunflower County. By the 1950s the program had been taken over by the Farm Security Administration and many of the tenants had paid for their forty acres and bought adjoining land for cotton crops. It was in one of these fields that Mae Bertha first met Fannie Lou Hamer, who had come on a truck from Ruleville. Picking cotton with Fannie Lou one day, Mae Bertha told her, "You pick the cleanest row of anybody."

"Everything I do, I try to do the best I can," was Fannie Lou's reply.

Mae Bertha later came to realize how prophetic those words were: Fannie Lou Hamer became one of the first blacks to register to vote in Sunflower County and a national figure in the Civil Rights Movement of the 1960s.

As she picked cotton on Sunflower Plantation, Mae Bertha was often bemused by working for white people who seemed poorer than she was. After going into the house of one of the resettlement families, she told Matthew, "That's what pride do. They won't pick their own cotton—rather pay us and don't even have a stove to cook on."

Mae Bertha thought that Matthew liked farming, but she worried because he got so tired. "All that labor," she said, "doing all that hard work and everything. Sometimes I wondered did he really like to farm or didn't have no other choice. I remember telling my husband so many times, 'I'll be glad when cotton goes out of business.' And Matthew would say, 'Don't say that, Mary, just say you'll be glad when you don't have to pick no more cotton,' and I'd say, 'Well okay, something like that.' See, he didn't want me to be sad—he wanted me to be happy and I was getting down, living on that farm with no hope, but see that's all he knew how to do at that time."

Nevertheless, Matthew Carter was a good farmer, proud of his labor.

He was considered a hard worker and his family got what was called "black people's respect." So the Carters worked and waited, not really sure what they were waiting for. They didn't realize they were waiting for a time, coming soon, that would change their lives and Drew and the Delta forever.

Amzie Moore's filling station, Cleveland, Mississippi, c. 1960.

Four

Let It Shine All Over the Delta

By 1961, the Delta's black community was talking about a young New Yorker named Bob Moses who had come south to join Amzie Moore during the summer of 1960. Willie Mae Johnson called Mae Bertha on the phone from Cleveland, Mississippi. She and Mae Bertha had been good friends for many years, as Johnson was active in the NAACP and in Cleveland's community activities. She said, "You got to come to these new mass meetings. These young people are really talking."

Moses, a teacher in the New York public school system, had been inspired by the black students who began the sit-in movement at a

Woolworth's lunch counter in Greensboro, North Carolina, on February 1, 1960. That summer he went to Atlanta, where he made friends with Jane Stembridge, the office secretary for the Student Nonviolent Coordinating Committee. The SNCC was a young people's civil rights group born out of the sit-ins and other nonviolent demonstrations that swept the South that spring. More than seventy thousand people participated in demonstrations after Greensboro; most of them were southern black college students, and SNCC represented their leadership. Stembridge and SNCC adviser Ella Baker, at the organization's Atlanta office, had suggested that Moses contact Amzie Moore. After moving to Cleveland, Moses wrote Stembridge back in Atlanta that Moore was "like a tree that's planted by the water."

In early 1961, young civil rights workers, committed to changing the lives of African-Americans in the South, were converging on Mississippi. They belonged to various organizations—the NAACP was no longer the only presence in the state. Medgar Evers of the NAACP admired the new organizers from SNCC and the Congress of Racial Equality (CORE), and, along with Bob Moses, he recognized the necessity of uniting these outside volunteers with the local Mississippi civil rights workers. To this end, in February 1962, the Council of Federated Organizations (COFO) was formed as a loose coalition. At first Amzie Moore and Moses talked about implementing one of Moore's long-deferred dreams—a voter registration drive in the Delta. But when Moses returned to Cleveland in the summer of 1961, Moore sensed the time was still not right for the campaign—perhaps because of a lack of local black support. So Moses went on to southwest Mississippi to work with local leaders preparing to launch an intensive voter education and registration campaign there.

The young volunteers, most of them affiliated with SNCC, moved into Mississippi towns to register voters. Many of them had dropped out of college to do this work, and in April 1962, several, including Diane Nash of SNCC and James Bevel of SCLC, came to Cleveland to work with Amzie Moore and Bob Moses to launch a new drive for voter registration in the Delta. Between 1961 and 1962, COFO's leadership caused new stirrings of hope in Mississippi's black community.

And then thirty-six-year-old Medgar Evers was murdered in Jackson. Shortly after midnight, on June 12, 1963, a rifle bullet shot him down in front of his house as he returned home from a rally at the New Jerusalem Baptist Church in Jackson. Earlier that evening, on national television, President Kennedy had described a bill he was sending to Congress—the bill that would become the Civil Rights Act of 1964. Evers's friends told of being with him that night and of how he led them in singing one of the movement songs, "This may be the last time"—lyrics that later seemed prescient.

Despite the assassination of Evers, and of Kennedy later that year, and in the face of mounting white opposition, the student organizers and local activists carried on. COFO leaders planned a major voter registration campaign first called the Mississippi Summer Project. The plan called not only for voter registration but also for opening freedom schools and community centers in thirty-one Mississippi communities. In June of 1964, a thousand volunteers from all over the United States gathered for the COFO-sponsored orientation program in Oxford, Ohio, and then crossed into Mississippi to launch the amazing effort that came to be known as Freedom Summer.

"ALL OVER the Delta, I'm gonna let it shine," sang the summer volunteers assigned to Sunflower County, on the final evening of orientation in Ohio, inspired by a young, handsome veteran activist named Charles McLaurin. The words would echo through Sunflower County all summer long. McLaurin had come to open the SNCC office in Ruleville, Mississippi, in 1962 and to take on the long, slow battle for voter education and registration of the 98 percent of the eligible black voters not on the Sunflower County rolls. The young people who crossed the Mississippi state line just south of Memphis drove into a world completely alien to them—most were white college students from upper-middle-class families.

One of the 1964 summer volunteers was Mike Yarrow, a twenty-four-year-old Quaker from Philadelphia. His father, Mike Yarrow, Sr., had been chairman of the AFSC Rights of Conscience Committee eight years earlier and was one of those responsible for sending the grant to Amzie Moore that helped him stay in business. The younger Yarrow later told me, "I remember the first day coming in from Memphis, Tennessee, to Ruleville. We ended up at Fannie Lou Hamer's house on a hot, hot Sunday, and she had a big pecan tree in the front yard. There were all these people gathered there, all these local people and press people and this whole group of volunteers who had just gotten there. And I mean it was the first time I took a deep breath and relaxed at all since I'd gotten across the border into Mississippi. In Ruleville, I lived with a black family and was going to those mass meetings every night in the church and walking through the neighborhoods, canvassing. Although it was pretty well organized by that time, there were still people who either hadn't gone to try to register or hadn't signed the freedom registration forms. People gradually did that. But there were some holdouts until after a while it felt comfortable enough. The black community felt united, solid. It felt like home, you know, it felt safe for them.

"But we were afraid to go to Drew. Twenty-six years later I still remember gritting my teeth, feeling like we were going into hostile territory. The first few times we went there, the police were coming through—we were starting to canvass in the black community up near the highway where the cotton fields come right up to the houses. They were so exposed, not many trees. Police and planters—or, anyway, white guys—rode around in pickup trucks glaring at us, taking pictures of us and the local people. The mothers were calling their kids away from talking to us, trying to protect them. We felt very like we were stirring up a hornets nest.

"I remember a proud World War I veteran with a wooden leg I talked to several times. He finally decided to go to Indianola to try to register to vote. He said he fought for freedom in the war and he hadn't seen any since and figured he was about to die and so he'd try this one thing. He forgot his glasses and maybe couldn't read very well, but he failed the literacy exam. But doing it was important to him.

"Drew was rough, but a few people from Drew started coming to Ruleville to mass meetings—some women, some older people, and some of the student-age kids. Then we tried to hold some rallies in Drew and got arrested. One kid who was arrested in Drew with us was on his way to football practice and just got enthused and ended up in jail. Pretty wild. The jail was near the railroad track, a little square cement-block building—it looked like one of those little power stations—just a hall and three or four cells.

"Sometimes I thought that the people in Ruleville were registering to vote or joining the movement because mechanization meant they weren't needed—they had no power in the old plantation relationship and their economic rights were eroding away. As black people were displaced from the plantations they moved into black areas in these little Delta towns where they lived on welfare or did day labor for three dollars a day—thirty cents an hour for a ten-hour day. I remember some of those laborers would get picked up in these rickety old open trucks to go to the fields, and some people got killed in a wreck getting tossed out of a truck. But they had a little community and their own church and maybe were a little more free. But for the people left on the plantations like the Carters—we never went near those plantations around Drew. They were private property. We were afraid of being arrested for trespassing, or that they would just shoot us."

Charles McLaurin also remembered Drew this way: "I had talked to a lot of people around Ruleville and one of the things they said was, 'Don't get caught in Drew. Don't cause problems in Drew.' Drew had a reputation for suppressing black men especially. I always felt that it was the hellholes that challenged us. If they were forbidden, I wanted to see why. If people said it couldn't be done, I wanted to try to prove it could. But Drew was tough—they just used real police tactics and violence and a lot of the people who wanted to register to vote—the white people constantly caused them problems until I believe they just left Drew."

One tool the organizers used in persuading people to register was the *Sunflower County Political Handbook,* a mimeographed and stapled booklet produced by the Freedom Information Service at Tougaloo College, near Jackson. The first page laid out the message for the black community:

WHAT POLITICS IS ALL ABOUT

Politics is about <u>our lives.</u>

It is about whether the roads are any good.

It is about what our kids learn in school.

It is about what the sheriff does.

It is about whether we have work to do.

Politics is about <u>who</u> has <u>power.</u>

The President listens to people who have power.

So does the Sheriff.

<u>Power</u> is <u>votes</u> to elect people, or not elect them.

<u>Power</u> is <u>money</u> to pay for election ads.

The people with power get what they want.

Now just a few people have <u>power</u>.

They get control of government money.

They get government contracts for their factories.

They get the tax assessor to list their land at a low value.

We do not have money.

Our power must come from <u>ourselves.</u> From our numbers.

From us being together.

We must have power for <u>us</u>.

So <u>we</u> control Sunflower County.

So the President listens to <u>us</u>.

So that we get what <u>we</u> need.

This is a book about how things work. It is a book about how <u>power</u>
is used to keep us <u>down</u>.

And how we can use power to lift ourselves <u>up</u>.

Another nice, direct message was lettered on the wall of the small house in the black section of Indianola that served as the Freedom Democratic party's headquarters:

There are rich people and poor people.
Middle class people are the same as rich people.
They have more things than they need.

These are the opening lines of a poem written by SNCC staffer Jane Stembridge.

Although organizing on the plantations was dangerous, some workers did venture onto them at night, and little by little sharecroppers began attending the mass meetings in Ruleville. On July 3, 1964, at one such meeting, Charles McLaurin introduced six people from Drew—the first ever to come from that town.

ON THURSDAY, July 30, 1964, the *Sunflower County News* carried a two-column editorial—"Time for Action!!"—which listed the "facts" about Communist involvement in the Civil Rights Movement and offered to give "Luther King the names of the known Communists in his movement." The article continued:

"It should be quite obvious the Communists would refrain from running through the streets with Red banners and waving Communist flags. This type of action would immediately unite the American public and would defeat their cause. Why not work through a movement sponsored by Council of Churches and have the protection of Federal Marshals, FBI Agents and the entire American armed services as their resources if they are needed?

The Negro public should be advised not to associate or otherwise affiliate or give comfort by word of mouth or deed with outside organizations. The Communists are not motivated by any honest desire to assist the Negro in this country, and strive only to advance the objectives of the Communist Party.

In August 1964, Drew's mayor, W. O. Williford, better known as "Snake" because of his ability to weave on the football field, wrote and distributed a leaflet claiming that "leftist lawyers were defending civil rights workers." He also proclaimed that "any civil rights worker found within the city limits at the close of a normal working day would be placed in jail 'for their own protection.'" Mayor Williford told me he was sincere about wanting to avoid violence; police brutality in a town long known for being a law unto itself had made him honestly fearful. He also wanted to avoid any large-scale civil rights activities in the town. And he succeeded. Surrounding towns were embroiled in clashes between COFO workers and local white people, but Drew remained relatively peaceful.

In retrospect, Mae Bertha and her family were glad they were living on the Pemble Plantation rather than in town in Drew during the heady days of the early 1960s freedom movement. For the Carters it was easy to go into Cleveland to attend the mass meetings and meet the young COFO workers. Mae Bertha told me later, "We'd go to those mass meetings at New Hope Baptist Church when those students came down here and I was so glad to go to them, I didn't know what to do. We'd hear young people like Julian Bond and John Lewis, and we'd start to singing all those good songs and I don't know, we just felt different and we'd just want to come out of the church and go do *something*."

Mae Bertha told me about one of the white volunteers who worked in Cleveland: "He opened my eyes to a lot of things. One time when we were at a mass meeting with this man, I really did fall in love with him. He came down here—said his daddy was a congressman. He'd make you feel so good and make us laugh—he had this accent, you know. He'd say, 'Now you're going out there in the field picking cotton for thirty cents an hour, and you know whites wouldn't get out in those hot fields if you were giving them ten dollars an hour.' So he would bring out some things like that, and I just loved him. Then, when he left and went back, I was so sad."

Twenty-five years later, when Mae Bertha was speaking to college students at the University of Virginia, a young white woman asked her how she now felt about those summer volunteers. Mae Bertha's body straightened and her voice rose, "Oh yes, oh yes, we loved them every one and we wish y'all would come down again right now. We still need you."

By the time Freedom Summer ended, six people had been killed, reportedly by Klansmen. There had been eighty reported beatings, thirty-five shootings, and sixty-eight bombings or burnings of black churches. Most of the summer volunteers returned to college, but COFO offices remained open in many towns, including Ruleville in Sunflower County and Cleveland in Bolivar County. Mae Bertha may have missed some of the summer volunteers after they went home, but to this day she is firm in her devotion to local leaders, "who were there before and stayed fighting after those other young people were gone. You take that Reverend Leroy Johnson in Cleveland. He was arrested and been in jail so many times and almost killed way before that summer."

Mae Bertha and I visited Leroy Johnson in Cleveland in 1992. He told me of his early voter registration work in 1962 and of one attempt on his life. He was working for the Coca-Cola Company at the time. One day, while carrying a case of Coke down a narrow alley, a beer truck driven by a white man came barreling down the alley toward him. He was treated for chest injuries caused by hugging the case of bottles close as he squeezed himself against the alley wall to avoid the truck. Soon after, he became chairman of the Bolivar County Mississippi Freedom Democratic party, and word got out that he had been in the march on Washington with Martin Luther King, Jr. After Coca-Cola fired him, he worked full-time for the Civil Rights Movement, usually without pay. He told Mae Bertha and me, "Fighting for freedom is like going to work every day." He was still working, still registering voters, when he died in 1993 at the age of fifty-two.

THE ENERGY of Freedom Summer helped strengthen the Carter family's will. First, in mid-May of 1965, Naomi Carter came home from New York City. Born in 1943, she was the Carters' third child and third daughter. She had graduated from Hunter High School in 1961 and left Mississippi in 1962 for Kansas City, where she lived for two years with her sister Edna. Then she had worked as a maid in New York City for a year. When she returned to Sunflower County in the summer of 1965, she married L.C. Granberry from Cleveland and renewed her friendship with Willie Mae Johnson's children and other young people who told her about Cleveland's civil rights activities and how the town had been a focal point of voter registration during Freedom Summer.

Ruth Carter, the next oldest child at home, also had friends in

Cleveland, and Naomi discovered that Ruth, too, was caught up by the exciting and infectious feel of "freedom in the air." Ruth remembers, "I was around fifteen and my mother's friend Willie Mae Johnson, in Cleveland, had a son, Arnester, and two daughters, Linda and Elnora, around my age. They would come and pick up me and my sister Naomi, and we would go to the mass meetings in Cleveland— like once a week. We listened to ideas and we would sing and we would pray. But what I remember the most about those days of the sixties was the songs—singing and dreaming of a better life."

Some of those dreams seemed to be growing real that summer in 1965. The Mississippi Freedom Democratic party had been formed in 1964 to challenge the Mississippi Democratic party over its lack of black representation. The Freedom party's lobbyists in Washington had publicized the violent response to Freedom Summer. That, along with the brutal suppression of the voting rights march in Selma, Alabama, in the spring of 1965—which was broadcast on national television—had almost ensured passage of the Voting Rights Act.

In early June 1965, Naomi went with Reverend Leroy Johnson and other young people from Cleveland to a workshop at the Highlander Center in Knoxville, Tennessee, where they joined groups from throughout the South. Highlander Center was founded in 1932 as the Highlander Folk School. In its early years, it provided educational support for the southern labor movement. By the fifties, Highlander had turned its attention to battling institutional racism, and in the sixties it conducted "citizenship schools" and workshops to teach African-Americans how to organize for social justice. In Naomi's workshop, the young people were taught the basic philosophy and tactics of nonviolent direct action and about organizing for voter education and registration. As soon as Johnson's group got back to Cleveland, they tested the public accommodations provisions of the Civil Rights Act by organizing a sit-in at Michael's Cafe on Highway 61. Ruth and Naomi were among those who sat at the tables. Everybody was served. No one was arrested.

As Johnson and his coworkers in Bolivar County prepared for another big voter registration drive, they received notice that Mississippi Governor Paul Johnson had called a special session of the state legislature to repeal discriminatory voting laws. At least that was the official reason. The real reason was devious: Johnson had no intention of ending the discriminatory voting and registration practices in Mississippi, but he hoped to protect the state from legal action on the part of civil rights activists by complying with the proposed voting rights bill before it became law. In Jackson, Lawrence Guyot, the chairman of the Freedom Democratic party, saw through the governor's plan and called for people from across the state to march with him in Jackson to protest the legislative session. Guyot claimed that holding the session violated federal law: because the Mississippi legislators were elected when most of the black people in the state couldn't vote, Guyot argued, the legislature was illegally constituted.

In the Delta, Guyot's call was answered by enough people to fill several buses to Jackson. Ruth, Naomi, and their friend Nettie Davis were on the bus from Cleveland. Ruth, as a minor, had to get her parents' permission. Matthew and Mae Bertha had given it but warned her that she might end up in jail. Ruth's solemn answer, Mae Bertha told me, was that at least she wouldn't be chopping cotton. The marchers stayed in a dormitory at Jackson State University the first night. The next morning, June 14, they gathered at Morning Star Baptist Church to mobilize for the mile-long walk in silence to the state capitol. Waiting for the group of five hundred demonstrators, nearly half of whom were teenagers, was one of the largest law enforcement contingents ever assembled in the capital. Jackson police—in full riot gear—halted the marchers and began arresting them for parading without a permit. Ruth and Naomi were among the 482 marchers arrested.

Ruth was terrified. "They put us in this paddy wagon," she recalled, "just one on top of the other until you couldn't get another person in the wagon and then they closed the door and closed all the windows. It was so hot. They just let us sit there, and we stayed in there for so long we thought we were going to pass out from the heat or else not make it out of there at all. This one lady started praying, and she prayed and prayed, and it was loud. We kept saying, 'Lady, please, if you stop praying, maybe they'll let us out of here.' Finally, they let us out and when we hit the air it actually felt cold, although it must have been ninety-five degrees.

"There were too many of us to put in the city jail, so they took us to the state fairgrounds where they kept the elephants. They set up type-writers and booked us one by one. They called us up and took our names and addresses and asked us whose plantation we lived on, so they could call the owner. It was something that I'll never forget."

The paddy wagons filled up quickly, so Reverend Johnson and other marchers were loaded into cotton trailers or large trash trucks. On the way to the fairgrounds, the police cars that were hauling the trailers sped and swerved so that the trailers swung dangerously from side to side on the roads.

Ruth described Johnson's retaliation: "When we came to stoplights we divided up on the sides of the trailers and rocked and rocked as hard as we could. Pretty soon, those old police cars and trucks that were hauling us started rocking themselves and lifting their back tires right off the ground. After that they didn't swing us."

The marchers were herded into the industrial and agricultural exhibit buildings on the fairgrounds, and some remained there for as long as three weeks. Although the July heat was intense, all of the buildings' furnaces were turned on and up. The marchers were made to go to bed very early and to share small bare mattresses with no cover. They were awakened at 5:30 A.M., the mattresses were removed, and the prisoners were left to sit on the cement floors. Some were afraid to go to sleep at night, and they sat up against the walls until morning. But always there was singing. Ruth's and Naomi's favorite was, "Before I'll be a slave, I'll be buried in my grave, and go home to my Lord and be free." Ruth said, "Sometimes in that jail, I thought I *would* be buried in my grave."

At times, Naomi was frightened as well. There were days when she truly doubted if she would get out alive. During the daylight hours, the police brought the marchers outside onto the fairgrounds and made them form rows; those in the front row had to stand along an imaginary line. The police said if they crossed the line, they would be hit with billy clubs. Once the prisoners were lined up, they were ordered to "move back," then "move up," "move back," "move up." Those in the front row inevitably crossed the imaginary line as they "moved up," and they were hit with flailing clubs. When the marchers were ordered back inside the buildings, the billy clubs waited for any stragglers. Naomi never got hit, but she watched a lot of people being beaten. She remembered that the police seemed especially furious at the young men with beards, whom they took outside of the jail to beat, yelling, "We'll have no damned Malcolm X around here."

These arrests and jailings took place a full year after the Civil Rights Act of 1964. By all accounts, they were among the most vicious and violent ever to occur in Mississippi. Even a pregnant woman was hit with clubs, and doctors were not allowed to visit prisoners who had been beaten. The Mississippi Freedom Democratic party appealed nationally for concerned people to come to Jackson to support voting rights. By the end of a two-week period, over one thousand other demonstrators had been arrested. But the nation's memory of Freedom Summer had faded; the shock of the murders of civil rights workers in Philadelphia, Mississippi, and Selma, Alabama, had eased; press coverage had all but stopped; and America was losing interest in Southern racism.

Back in Drew, Mae Bertha and Matthew saw the televised reports on the mass arrests and incarceration at the Jackson fairgrounds. When a frantic Mae Bertha managed to get to the police headquarters at the fairgrounds, officials told her that the marchers were "doing okay—they were having fun and would be out soon." Mae Bertha persisted, saying that Ruth was a minor and she had come to take her home. Finally, after five days, Ruth was released.

"When I got to the fairground—ooh, they was singing some songs and they were still happy," Mae Bertha told me. "They was happy! They were singing, 'I'm gonna do what the spirit say do. If the spirit say march, we're going to march on off, we're gonna do what the spirit say do.'

"And when I was about to go in, this here man started talking down to me saying, 'Now don't you let your children run off and come back down here anymore.' I said, 'Look, my children did not run off to come down here. They asked me to let them come down here and I let them come, and if I hadn't had more children at home I would've come with them.'

"So Ruth came out of a big building. She was so dirty, clothes all filthy, hadn't had a bath in five days. All they had to eat was lye hominy and cold grits. And they didn't have no secret place to go to the bathroom. Naomi stayed eleven days and she hadn't had a bath since she'd been down there."

Mae Bertha wasn't afraid during the days that she waited for Ruth and Naomi to be released. As in the past, "a kind of covering" came over her that made her feel sure everything would be all right. When she heard the singing as she reached the fairgrounds, she felt it more strongly. She would experience the "covering" many times in the months and years to come whenever she most needed it.

On August 6, 1965, Congress passed the Voting Rights Act. The law prohibited discriminatory practices that had been long used to keep blacks from registering to vote, and it enabled the U.S. attorney general to send federal registrars into counties with a history of such discrimination. On the day the bill was passed, only 1 percent of Sunflower County's African-Americans were registered to vote, though they made up 60 percent of the population. Mae Bertha was counted in that 1 percent, and she cried when she heard that the act had passed. "So we really was in the movement," she told me later. "Going to these mass meetings and marching and going to jail and singing and talking about you ain't gonna let nobody turn you 'round. So that's why we was already motivated when the school integration came."

Part II

Sunflower Seeds

Sunflower River.

Slaughter family, Smith and Wiggins Plantation, c. 1908.
Mae Bertha's father, Isaiah Slaughter, back right.

Five

A Nice-Lookin' Li'l Ole Boy

Anyone who knows Mae Bertha will soon see that her devotion to her children and her belief in the importance of education came down to her from her mother, Luvenia Noland Slaughter. When I asked Luvenia where Mae Bertha got the courage to make the choices she did, Luvenia didn't hesitate. "Well," she said, "she got that from me." I met Luvenia for the first time in 1991, just before her eighty-ninth birthday. This remarkable smaller version of light-skinned, blue-eyed Mae Bertha told me her story with the same asperity and clarity of vision that she has passed on to her daughter.

75

TO FIVE-year-old Luvenia Noland, the Sunflower River seemed like paradise. Pecan, mulberry, and plum trees lined the banks, and tall wild sunflowers swayed gently in the breeze as they turned their gold-and-brown faces to the passing sun. The river water was wide, deep, and swirling, fed by cold shallow streams that invited children to drink.

Luvenia was born on August 12, 1903, in Wilkinson County, a part of Mississippi the natives consider the state's hill country. Cotton was hard to raise there under the best of circumstances, but after 1908, the year boll weevils first struck, it became virtually impossible. Lured by stories of the Mississippi Delta—soil as fertile as land along the Nile, an endless growing season, enormous cotton crops, and plenty of work—Mary and William Noland and their daughters, Delsie and Luvenia, migrated north in 1908 to Sunflower County.

The Nolands' destination was Birch Plantation on the east bank of the Sunflower River. Mary Noland's mother, Eliza Smith Fields, was sharecropping there and took the Nolands into her three-room house. Three months later, Eliza and her immediate family left the crowded house and moved to another one on the plantation. Luvenia and Delsie remained with their parents in the three-room house near the river.

Two years before the Nolands arrived in Sunflower County, local plantation owners had built a ferry to cross the river. Big enough to transport passengers, wagons and buggies, horses, mules and oxen, and even an occasional car, the ferry was a wooden raft with railings on two sides and aprons that opened on either end to allow passengers on and off. Strong cables looped around a tree on one bank and stretched across the river to a tree on the opposite bank. Travelers used the cable to pull themselves hand over hand, back and forth, across the river.

The ferry was not far from the Nolands' house on Birch Plantation, and it crossed the river to Smith and Wiggins's land on the opposite bank. To plantation children, who called the ferry the floating bridge, it was a source of constant activity and excitement. Luvenia's parents allowed her to pull the ferry across the river if she recognized the waiting passengers on the opposite bank. Nickels and dimes for this service, and from selling pecans that dropped from trees on the riverbanks, provided Luvenia with pocket money during her childhood.

Mary and William Noland joined Mary's mother sharecropping on Birch's vast acres of cotton and corn. Like most of the large Delta plantations, Birch was almost self-sufficient. The cotton gin, the plantation doctor's office, the business office, the commissary, and the barn, which housed one hundred mules, were all close to Luvenia's house by the river. At the Birch dock, the steamboats unloaded supplies for the plantation and took on cottonseed and barrel staves at one cent per ton to carry downriver to Vicksburg. As was the custom, all the buildings on the plantation, including the sharecroppers' cabins, were painted the Birch colors—a dark red with white trim.

Birch Plantation was owned by railroad interests in the Midwest and managed by local white residents. When Luvenia was growing up, Birch was run by Ed Pemble from nearby Merigold. As a young man, Pemble had been employed as bookkeeper and was known to the workers for keeping the books "straight" and for trying to give the sharecroppers their fair share of earnings at settlement time. Eventually Pemble accumulated his own enormous cotton acreage in Sunflower County, including the land on which Mae Bertha and Matthew were living in 1965.

Luvenia and Delsie went to school first at the home of a neighbor who was paid by their mother to teach them their ABCs. Two years later they started school at the Pleasant Green Church on the plantation. In the early days of public education in Mississippi, black churches on plantations were designated as the schools for black children from the surrounding area. At Pleasant Green Church there was one room and one teacher, who taught reading to children through the fifth grade. Luvenia attended school on a split-session schedule, for a total of four or five months at the most each year, depending entirely on the vicissitudes of the cotton-growing season.

Ten miles away from Birch Plantation, in Bolivar County, was Mound Bayou, an all-black community founded in 1887 that to this day advocates economic independence, quality education, and lives of dignity for African-Americans. Luvenia remembered with pride the trips she took there and how she was terribly disappointed in 1912 when she didn't get to go with some of her friends to Mound Bayou to hear Booker T. Washington at the opening of the Mound Bayou Oil Mill, a black-owned enterprise and the first of its kind in the Delta.

Luvenia's sister, Delsie, became very ill at the age of twelve. She started bleeding from the mouth and died after two days. Luvenia's mother told her it had to do with Delsie's entering womanhood. Friends came from the surrounding plantations to mourn the young girl and to see her buried in the blacks' cemetery near Pleasant Green Church. The day of Delsie's funeral was the day that eight-year-old Luvenia met her future husband. After the burial, Luvenia went down to the ferry alone. There, on the opposite bank, she saw for the first time a ten-year-old boy named Isaiah Slaughter. Zeke, as they called him, was playing with Tom and Frank and other boys who lived near the river. Their games were interrupted when Tom's mother told him to take the family's small boat to get some kerosene at the commissary over on Birch. As he rowed back across the river with the kerosene, the other boys hollered to him to meet them at the ferryboat landing. When Tom pulled his little boat up to the landing, Frank jumped into it with a laugh. Luvenia stood on the bank and watched in horror as the boat sank and Tom, unable to swim, drowned in the swift river waters. Curled up on the riverbank, she cried until her mother found her and carried her to Grandmother Eliza's house, away from the river. Luvenia stayed there for several months. For a year after she came home, she would offer her daddy her nickels and dimes if he would let her get in her parents' bed when storms came and the river rose, reminding her of Delsie and Tom, buried a day apart on either side of the Sunflower River.

But on sunny days she thought of Zeke and told her mother about the "nice-lookin' li'l ole boy" she had seen on the other side of the river that day. "I don't know why, I liked him at first eyesight. He just looked good to me." And on those sunny days, Luvenia would stand on the riverbank by her house hoping to catch another glimpse of him over on Smith and Wiggins's land.

Unlike the absentee owners of Birch Plantation, J. R. Smith and A. B. Wiggins lived nearby, in Merigold, just over the line in Bolivar County. By 1906 most of the densely wooded lands in the Delta had been cleared and the open land had been cultivated and consolidated into large plantations. The Smith and Wiggins partnership was prominent among the first large white landowning interests in the area. Smith and Wiggins rented a few parcels of land to black families that could afford the rent, but their huge cotton, corn, and bean crops were raised and harvested primarily by sharecroppers.

Zeke's father, Jeff Slaughter, had worked as a sharecropper and managed to save enough money to buy mules, then a wagon, and the other necessities that ultimately allowed him to rent land from Smith and Wiggins. Along with his wife, Julia, their nine children, and a couple of sharecropping families of his own, Jeff farmed sixty acres of cotton.

Zeke was the oldest of the Slaughter children, and the year after Luvenia first saw him at the river, they both started going to the Hyde Bayou School at White Chapel Church on the Smith and Wiggins Plantation. Every day after school, Zeke carried Luvenia's books down the road to the ferry turnoff where she crossed the river to go home.

When Luvenia was twelve, her parents sent her to school at the Southland Institute, just outside West Helena, Arkansas. Southland was the first permanent educational institution for blacks west of the Mississippi, and it offered both elementary and secondary curricula. In 1866, the men of the 56th Colored Regiment, who were stationed at Helena, bought thirty acres of land near their camp and deeded it to the Indiana Yearly Meeting of Friends. Under the determined leadership of the Quaker abolitionists Calvin and Alida Clark, Southland was established on the site as a school for freedmen, particularly for lost and abandoned black children. Despite hostility from the white community, and despite drought, disease, and floods, the school endured, offering science, mathematics, natural history, bookkeeping, German, and Latin. Southland diplomas were recognized by the Arkansas board of education.

When they heard about Southland, Mary and Will Noland began to scrimp and save. In the fall of 1915, twelve-year-old Luvenia crossed the Mississippi River for the first time as she headed for Southland,

along with several other children from Birch Plantation. At the institute, students from out of state lived in dormitories and were taught
for a full nine months each year by white teachers from the North.
Luvenia learned more during her first year than she ever had before,
but a yellow fever epidemic was raging in the Delta when she came
home in early summer, and in September, the children who had
accompanied her the previous year were still too sick to leave. William
and Mary were afraid to send Luvenia by herself, so she stayed home
and joined them in the fields. For the rest of her life she sang the songs
she had learned at Southland. It was the last of her schooling. Southland survived ten more years before closing from lack of funds.

ON A Sunday night in September 1919, when Zeke was eighteen and
Luvenia sixteen, the two slipped away after church and got married in
Whitney, a tiny whistle-stop nine miles from Birch Plantation. Marriage to Zeke was what Luvenia wanted, and she says she added the
words "I ain't never loved nobody but Zeke" to their vows. The next
morning they set out on foot back to Birch.

Zeke left Luvenia with her parents while he went across the river to
tell his own family. At sundown he came back to fetch her. "Come on,
Luvenia, my mama's left the cotton fields early to go home to cook
dinner for your coming to the family." Luvenia left with him a little
reluctantly. She had been good friends with Zeke's sister Annie, who
was her age, but Annie had died of yellow fever just a week before
Luvenia married Zeke. Except for Annie and one brother from her
school, Luvenia didn't know the Slaughters. Moreover, she was afraid
of Jeff Slaughter from the stories she had heard of his "snappish" ways.

When they arrived, the table was set, and Luvenia sat down with

Julia and Jeff Slaughter and their children. She couldn't eat and Zeke told his daddy that Luvenia was afraid of him.

"What you scared of me for, girl? I ain't gonna bite you," he said. The Slaughters told Luvenia to call them Mama and Papa, and they loved her as they did their own children. Julia said, "The Lord done sent me another daughter."

The Slaughters' house had five rooms and was newly built on the Smith and Wiggins Plantation. Zeke and Luvenia stayed there until March 1920, when Luvenia was three months pregnant. Their new home was only a few yards away from Jeff and Julia's. Through the first spring and summer of their marriage, Zeke farmed for his father while Luvenia put the new house in order, tended the garden plot that Jeff had given them, and awaited the arrival of their firstborn. She had not had sex before she married and in fact waited three months after the wedding to consummate the marriage. The first time she "gave over" to Zeke she got pregnant. She had no idea what to expect during pregnancy or childbirth. The teenage Luvenia weighed only ninety pounds when L.C. was born on August 15, 1920. Her mother, her mother-in-law, Zeke, and a midwife were all there for the birth. Julia Slaughter held one leg and Zeke the other.

Zeke hollered, "Don't you close your legs."

The midwife hollered, "If you close in, you'll kill it." Luvenia was in labor all night and long into the next day. She says it felt like an elephant was coming out and like she was being torn in two.

The midwife made a sugar tit for the baby to suck until Luvenia's milk came down. Within a few hours the little boy started screaming and straining and bleeding from his bowels and twenty-four hours later he was dead. Usually a sugar tit consisted of a little butter and sugar tied up in a piece of cheesecloth, but both Julia and Mary swore that the midwife took some cornbread off the stove and put it into the sugar tit. They believed that adding the cornbread killed L.C. His two grandmothers mourned his passing more deeply than did sixteen-year-old Luvenia.

Ten months later, on June 17, 1921, the birth of Charles Henry Slaughter (C.H.) was an entirely different story. Luvenia went into labor in the middle of a hot June night and asked Zeke to fetch his mother, Julia, from next door. "Mama's too tired, she went to church last night," he said. "I went to church last night, too," Luvenia shot back. "Now go get her."

Julia sent Zeke to get the midwife and at Luvenia's instruction made a pallet on the cool porch and placed a chair with a pillow on it at one end of the pallet. Luvenia knelt with her arms and head on the chair and her knees on the pallet.

"Mama, I'm hurtin' so, please rub my back," she said, and when Julia rubbed too gently, Luvenia told her to rub hard and bear down. Luvenia pushed a little bit and the baby came squalling into the moonlight.

"Oh my God," said Julia, "what are we gonna do now? Where's that midwife?"

"I don't know," Luvenia told her, "but I'm gonna rest right now if you can go in and fix my bed." Luvenia stayed on her knees for a few minutes, then rose slowly, with Julia lifting up the still-attached baby, and took the steps to her bed. The midwife came and told Luvenia she and Zeke had a big healthy boy. She helped Luvenia with the afterbirth and cut the umbilical cord, and by the time Zeke walked in the door, Luvenia and the baby were both comfortable in the bed. He told Luvenia he had been lagging behind the midwife praying, "Please,

God, let Luvenia done have that baby by the time I get back home." In the years to come, Luvenia would give birth to each of her twelve other children as she had to C.H.—on her knees.

By 1922, Jeff Slaughter was not able to save enough money to keep renting land from Smith and Wiggins and he had to go back to regular sharecropping, which brought the overseer or "rider" back into his family's life. Riders were hired by plantation owners or managers to oversee the crops from the planting of the first seed to the picking of the last tuft of cotton. Upon them rested the responsibility for producing the greatest number of cotton bales to generate the greatest profits for the landowners. Riders were, in general, ominous and threatening as they sat astride their horses or mules, looking down to cajole, goad, and intimidate.

Luvenia told me that Jeff Slaughter took one look at the newly hired rider in 1922 and thought to himself, "Smith and Wiggins must've picked him up out of the road." One day during planting season, when Zeke was working in a far field and Luvenia was chopping cotton near their house, she saw the rider coming toward her on his mule.

"Whoa," the rider said to the mule, and stopped where he could look straight down on Luvenia. "This evening I want you to take your hoe and go over there across the field and replant that cotton. Right there in front of that house where the people have walked it down."

"Yeah," Luvenia said, never looking up. When the rider was gone, she went to find Zeke.

The rider had broken the rules, she told Zeke. "He ain't got no business telling me nothing. I ain't no head of no crops or nothing. If he's going to tell anybody anything, he should have been telling you." In the old sharecropper system, the male sharecropper was the person responsible to the manager or owner, and the riders, managers, and owners did not have the right to give orders to other members of the family. This was a jealously guarded freedom. A few days later, Luvenia, two months pregnant, was inside her house when again the rider came across the field. She hurried outside with her hoe and vigorously began digging up cabbages in the family garden. "Whoa, mule," he said. Luvenia says she remembers thinking, "If he tries to get off that mule and do something to me, I'm gonna kill him with this hoe."

"Did you go over and replant that cotton like I told you?" he asked.

Luvenia can remember her anger to this day. "No, I did not. You ain't got no business telling me what to do no way. I ain't made no bargain with you. You're supposed to tell my husband, and if my husband wants me to do it, then I might do it."

"Well, I'll go see Zeke, see if he can't do something about you." He rode off on his mule and Luvenia called out after him. "Let me tell you one thing. Zeke can't make me do no more than I want to do." Luvenia swears that the baby in her womb stirred for the first time at that moment.

Whatever Zeke told the rider, it was the last Luvenia heard about replanting the cotton. That rider soon earned a reputation among the black sharecroppers for his meanness. On the last Saturday in August, Zeke went into Merigold to Smith and Wiggins's store to get his last "furnishing"—the feed, fertilizer, implements, food, and supplies that the sharecroppers received on credit from the plantation store just before picking time. The rider was in the store telling Zeke and the others that they better hurry up because he'd soon be out in the fields goading them to get that cotton picked. What the rider evidently didn't know was that Zeke and some other workers had gone to Mr. Smith and told him about this man's mistreatment. That same Saturday evening, Smith and Wiggins fired the rider.

"They put his butt back out in the road," Zeke told Luvenia.

Five months later, on January 13, 1923, Luvenia gave birth to her first daughter, Mae Bertha.

It seemed to Luvenia that she was pregnant all the time during the next few years. Julia was born in 1925. Robert was born in 1926 but was lost to pneumonia at eighteen months. Jesse Lee came in 1928, and Leroy in 1930.

At the age of six or seven, each child, starting with C.H. and Mae Bertha, had to help Zeke and Luvenia pick cotton at harvest time. As the children grew old enough to hold a hoe, they followed their parents to chop weeds during the growing months. When they were not working in the fields, Mae Bertha and her brother went to White Chapel Church to attend school. Sometimes the children would stop at the narrow stream of water called Hyde Bayou to play under the bridge and catch crawfish, which they proudly took home for Luvenia to cook for supper.

Occasionally Jeff Slaughter harnessed his mule and wagon, or his buggy—a rare possession for sharecroppers—to take his grandchildren into Merigold, nine miles away. This was always an exciting and much anticipated event, for Merigold was the hub of county activity. Here Mae Bertha and her brothers and sisters gazed at the bustle of the railroad depot. They admired the displays of food and cloth in the stores and watched the mail carriers pick up and deposit letters and packages at the Merigold post office. They stared at wagons full of cotton waiting by the towering, noisy machinery of the cotton gin and saw what happened to the small flour sacks of cotton they had picked. On the long ride home, they watched the sun set over their world of endless fields.

For all its isolation, rural Mississippi was not a peaceful place for African-Americans in the 1920s and 1930s. Maintaining the racial status quo was, of course, not the province of official law enforcement agencies alone. Most white people found it necessary and acceptable, if not routine, to form posses or "mob crews" to apprehend black "criminals" and act as judge, jury, and executioner. The "crime" might be a transgression against unspoken laws or against the social order. Between 1900 and 1941, 528 black people were lynched in Mississippi, the most of any state. In 1930, Luvenia's brother-in-law became one of that number.

Luvenia's half sister Liz was married to a man named Son Hampton. Called Son Ham, he and Liz lived on Sunflower Plantation across the river from Smith and Wiggins. Son Ham was down in Shaw, in Bolivar County, playing cards with a group of friends, when the police burst in on the game. A white policeman was shot. Son Ham said that he didn't do the shooting, but no matter—a mob crew had formed to kill all the men in the card game to make sure it got the right one. The crew drove to Son Ham's house on Sunflower. He wasn't there. They went to his mother's house, and because they didn't know Son Ham, they took his ten-year-old nephew in the car to help identify him. Son Ham was playing cards at a table down by the river behind the commissary on Birch Plantation. When he was told that the mob crew was driving up to the commissary, he ran to a friend's house. They locked the doors and waited. When the crew surrounded the house, Son Ham ran to the back, ducked through a window, crossed the porch, and ran into the fields. He hid in some high corn. As the crew got closer, he broke from the corn and ran across an empty field. His white pursuers shot him down as he ran.

Luvenia heard the shots all the way across the river on Smith and Wiggins. It was a Saturday evening and she thought it must be some folks out bullfrog hunting on the river. Soon after, though, Zeke came home with blood all over him. "Veenie, they shot Son Ham down like a rabbit. They made us go get his body and put it on the car. And Mr. Pemble came up and told that mob crew to get off his land."

The mob crew did leave, but with Son Ham's body in a cotton sack, tied like a deer to the front fender of a Model T. They drove the body through Merigold, Cleveland, and Shaw, so everyone would see Mississippi justice. They took the body back to Sunflower Plantation, dug a hole six feet deep, as required by law, and threw it in, filthy, blood-spattered clothes and all. They covered the spot so carefully that his family never was able to find it.

For years, when Zeke took Mae Bertha to see her grandmother on Birch Plantation, he would point to the field. "Right in that field, a mob crew shot Son Ham down like a rabbit. When they shot him, it blew the hat right off his head. No one would even go pick up poor old Son Ham's hat. The people were too afraid. That hat, it just blew and blew across the fields."

Living with constant indignities and the threat of violence was difficult for Zeke. He was the oldest son in a large family that had money and relative independence. Now he had a family of his own and a new child arriving almost every year. Before him stretched nothing but the thralldom of the cotton fields and a life of hard work. And every spring the vicissitudes of the Sunflower and Mississippi rivers threatened his crops. During the great flood of 1927, water surged through forty-two major levee breaks and covered more than thirty thousand square miles of land, including much of Sunflower County. Zeke, like many others who worked the land, was tempted by stories of opportunity elsewhere. He caught the train in Merigold and headed for Chicago. He told Luvenia to be ready to go—he would send for the family as soon as he got a job. He was back within two weeks, however. Luvenia suspected that one reason he returned was a woman named Florida Sharkey.

Florida was light brown, younger, taller, and bigger than Luvenia. Florida had liked Zeke when they were all in school, and Luvenia knew that Zeke was seeing Florida even after she and Zeke were married. Florida often gave Zeke money and bought him clothes and presents. She also stole clothes from a Merigold store for Mae Bertha and the other children and sent them home with Zeke. Luvenia hated to accept the clothing, but the children needed it. She also hated Florida, who would come and sit in front of Luvenia's fire in a bright red sweater, talking and joking with the children. At one point, Zeke was giving Florida three nights a week, Luvenia three, and keeping one for himself. Mae Bertha was aware of all this, and one day when Florida cut through their yard to a neighbor's house, she heard her mother scream out to Florida never to set foot on their land again. Mae Bertha remembers turning to her brother and saying to him, "When I grow up, I'm surely gonna kill that woman."

Finally, Luvenia told Zeke, "Go. We can't live together no longer. I am not going to live in this kind of a mess. You may be Jack, but I sure ain't none of Martha Ann or Emily." Jack lived down the road, had two wives and two sets of kids, and they all lived together. "I am not going to be in no partnership with no woman with my husband. Now go. I'll take these kids and do the very best I can for them."

Zeke put on two pairs of underwear, two pairs of socks, then pants, a shirt, and a jacket, and he left. He took no suitcase. He thought he would be back.

It was December 1931, the middle of the Great Depression. Luvenia had five children to care for and was pregnant. The first thing she did after Zeke left was pick up the baby and go to her mother-in-law.

"Mama Julia, Zeke's gone. I come down here to tell you that I am pregnant. I don't want folks be saying that I got pregnant with another man after Zeke left home. So I am telling you now. I love that man. Couldn't nobody love a man like I love Zeke, but I'm sick of it."

"Well, Luvenia," Julia said, "I birthed him, but I didn't know I birthed such a lowdown bastard."

Luvenia returned home to her children. She felt like a burden had been lifted from her. Although she continued to swear her love for Zeke, and although he asked her many times, she never took him back.

Mae Bertha Carter's mother, Luvenia Slaughter.
Belle Parker's Place, Sunflower County, c. 1940.

Six

I've Got Needs

A sharecropper's steady habits and devotion to the land could not protect him against bad weather, or the whims of landowners, or the cruelty of the law. Three months after Zeke left, Smith and Wiggins, feeling the bite of the Depression, sold the land that Luvenia's father-in-law, Jeff Slaughter, was sharecropping. In exchange for allowing him to continue living in his home and working the land, the new owners insisted that Jeff give up his mules, buggy, and wagon, to ensure his dependency. Jeff decided to stay on, but Luvenia and her children moved to another parcel of Smith and Wiggins's land, near Renova, ten miles away, between Merigold and Cleveland.

Before she moved, Zeke came to Luvenia to convince her to stay near his parents, who loved her like their own child.

"I'm moving," she told him, and a few minutes later the wagon rolled up. Luvenia had her own shotgun now, given to her by her father just before he died. She told Zeke to take his gun and the rest of his clothes. With a new sense of independence and determination to keep her five children together, she moved into the Renova house. Her best friend, Mary Jenkins, and Mary's baby, Billy, moved in with them, and Luvenia's mother, Mary, was in a house just down the road.

Smith and Wiggins's land at Renova was known locally as the Deadening, because as far as the eye could see the land was dotted with large tree stumps. During the twenties and thirties lumber and paper corporations moved through the Delta systematically cutting down trees. Plantation owners then hired sharecroppers and wage laborers to turn the devastated acreage into wealth-producing cotton crops.

During their first season at the Deadening, when Luvenia's pregnancy often kept her from the fields, eleven-year-old C.H. and nine-year-old Mae Bertha supported the family by chopping and picking cotton for thirty cents an hour. They tried but failed to pick a hundred pounds a day, the goal commonly set for each picker. The little money they brought home each day bought staples, which were cheap thanks to Depression prices—two or three cents a pound for sugar and flour. When Luvenia entered the final days of her pregnancy, she left the fields altogether to stay home and care for the younger children and her friend Mary's baby. She envied young Mary, who would go into nearby Cleveland to have fun on Friday and Saturday nights.

Ida Mae was born in August 1932. Luvenia tells the story that just before she gave birth, Smith and Wiggins wanted to go and find Zeke to bring him back. They told Luvenia to say the word and they'd see to it that Florida didn't bother her again.

"No," Luvenia told them. "I won't make nobody stay with me. If they don't want me, I don't want them." Luvenia says she knew very well that the owners also wanted Zeke's labor in their fields and were trying to use family ties as a means of persuasion. But there must have been admiration for Luvenia herself, too. Mr. Smith made Luvenia promise that as soon as she went into labor she would send into Merigold for the doctor and then make sure he got the bill. Ida Mae was Luvenia's first child to be delivered by a doctor.

That winter at the Deadening was a bad one for Luvenia and her children. Often there was no money to buy wood for cooking on the stove or for burning in the fireplace. She told me that it started to snow just before Thanksgiving and snowed for a week. The Friday and Saturday before the snow started, Luvenia took C.H. and Mae Bertha with her into the fields. They collected uprooted stumps and tree roots, put them in old cotton sacks, and dragged them home. Then they gathered dried cotton and cornstalks and stacked them with the wood on the long L-shaped porch of their house. Luvenia told the children that the Lord had told her to do it. When the storm came, it snowed and sleeted until the fields and levees and bayous were covered by a two-foot-deep blanket of white that spread over the endless flat land of the Delta as far as anyone could see. Luvenia had never seen anything like it and she thought the world was coming to an end. The snow was so high and the air so cold that water froze in the ground. When there was no more wood to build a fire to heat water for melting the snow around the pump, Luvenia brought bowls of snow inside to melt to use for water. Her ingenuity and faith in herself, along with the hard labor of C.H. and Mae Bertha, got them through.

Eating in winter depended on summer preparation. On Saturdays the summer before, Luvenia, Mae Bertha, and C.H. had picked field peas, dried them, put them in croker sacks, and hung them in the kitchen. That winter Luvenia would put the dried peas and some meat on the stove and let them cook all night. In the morning when the peas were done, she cooked cornbread at the fireplace and boiled sweet potatoes in the large black kettle. The little meat they had came from three hogs they had killed. There had been no money for corn for the hogs, so they had been fed on weeds and water. They were as poor and thin as could be, and their meat was sticky from lack of salt for curing. Luvenia made meal mush and dumplings with salt pork, or dressing without chicken called "cush," or cornbread crumbled up and seasoned with onion and black pepper. After the food was cooked, Luvenia fed the children their meal for that day in their beds so they could stay warm, covered with quilts and whatever worn-out cotton sacks she had been able to save.

Luvenia farmed, cared for the children, sewed, and cleaned. Although she scrimped and saved, she was at the end of her strength and her resources by the fall of 1934. Facing the fact that she needed more support, Luvenia agreed to live with another sharecropper, Willie Boyd. The news upset her mother-in-law, Julia.

"Luvenia, you just won't let well do," Julia said when her daughter-in-law told her what she planned to do.

"Look, Mama Julia, don't be puffing with me," Luvenia said. "Zeke's been gone two years. Left me with these kids. Ain't done nothing for them. He's heard I'm moving in with Willie Boyd. He's mad about that."

"You don't know how that new man is gonna treat those children."

This was the only time that Luvenia ever got mad with her mother-in-law. "I've got needs, Mama, I've got needs. I hope I'll be all right." Two days later she moved in with Willie Boyd on Belle Parker's farm, still in Sunflower County.

Zeke had also tried to talk her out of the move. He told her that he still loved her and wanted her back. Luvenia steadfastly refused. Even after Luvenia had children in her common-law marriage to Willie Boyd, Zeke told her, "You are my wife and always will be. Willie Boyd ain't got no kids." And in fact, Zeke's family treated all of Luvenia's children as if they were indeed Zeke's. She would stay on with Willie Boyd for ten years.

Luvenia later told her mother-in-law, "Zeke's the only man I've ever loved. I am with Willie Boyd because without him me and my kids would've starved to death. I got some kids for him but I never was his wife."

IN 1930, Captain Bonny Parker's neck was broken when his horse bolted from the ferry to the landing on the Sunflower River. Belle, his wife of thirty years, decided to run their 160-acre farm by herself. Her neighbors and the workers on her place called her Widow Belle Parker. Her sister, Emma Talley, lived with her from time to time, and their brother, Judge James Parker, came over from Arkansas occasionally, usually at settlement time. Small in comparison with the big plantations that surrounded it in Sunflower County, the Parker farm was located east of the Sunflower River, halfway between Drew and Cleveland.

Belle Parker had hired Willie Boyd to take care of her hogs and mules, as well as to help her farm, and she paid him a monthly salary of twenty-five dollars, a lot of money at a time when the going wage in the cotton fields was thirty-five cents a day. His house was next door to hers.

Boyd had a Model T and began buying groceries and taking them to Luvenia even before she moved into the house with him at Belle Parker's. When Luvenia and the children settled into his house, Luvenia sharecropped her own parcel on the plantation, in addition to washing clothes and cleaning house for Belle Parker. Willie Boyd ate his meals at Belle Parker's and brought leftover food to Luvenia and the children. It was the first winter in a long time that they were not hungry.

Belle Parker's neighbors thought her unusual. Even before her husband died, she often rode her horse through the fields and took part openly in running the farm. Five feet tall with long white hair that hung below her knees, she was a rather remarkable figure to Luvenia and her older daughters. She strode across the fields to the share-cropper cabins to visit, long hair flying behind her. In summer months she wore a bonnet, gloves, and long sleeves to protect her skin from the sun. She came to Luvenia's cabin frequently and made no bones about how much she liked both Luvenia and Mae Bertha. Mae Bertha and her sister Julia churned butter each morning in Belle's kitchen, and Belle often cooked their breakfasts—"the best biscuits in the world." As the three of them ate, they would discuss many subjects, but Belle Parker's favorite topic was religion.

Mae Bertha had been baptized in a long and complicated process at age twelve. On the day of her baptism, she went first to the "moaning bench" at Union Grove Baptist Church and prayed on her knees. She then went home but did not eat anything all day. At some point during the fasting ritual, Belle Parker noted that Mae Bertha was not eating her usual breakfast and asked about it.

"I'm trying to get religion and not supposed to eat nothing," Mae Bertha said.

Mrs. Parker finally convinced her that eating breakfast would not compromise her entry into the Kingdom.

In the afternoon, Mae Bertha went to the "praying ground" near the river and then back to the church, where the preacher and the church sisters prayed for her.

At a certain point, Mae Bertha said, "I got it now. I got the good religion."

"How you know you got it?" returned the sisters.

"I can feel it burning in my heart, I can see a shooting star," said Mae Bertha. She had been without food for most of the day. Then Mae Bertha went down to the Sunflower River, and with all the church members watching, the preacher immersed her in the water.

THREE MONTHS after Luvenia moved to Belle Parker's, Julia Slaughter sent word to Luvenia asking to see her grandchild Ida Mae. Ida Mae was one year old by then, but Jeff and Julia Slaughter had never seen her. Julia sent two of her sons to bring the baby back for an extended stay. The following week, while the other children were at school, Luvenia was sitting at home with Leroy, the youngest after Ida Mae, when something told her she should get up and wash clothes. She thought, no telling what was going to happen. She borrowed a big washtub from her neighbor and filled both it and her own tub behind the house.

Luvenia had the family's clothes in all stages of washing, rinsing, and drying when she heard someone say, "Whoa." It was a neighbor from Renova on his horse. "Your mama is just as sick as she can be," he said. Luvenia said she'd be off as soon as she could get the house in order and make arrangements for the children. She threw clothes on the line, straightened the house, and fixed dinner for the children. When Willie Boyd came home at noon, he told her to go ahead to her mother's, that he would take care of the children. When the children got home from school, Luvenia told them, "Your dinner's on the stove. I gotta go see about your grandma. She's as sick as she can be. I don't know when I'll be back. You're gonna have to take Leroy to school with you. I've nowhere to leave him."

Luvenia was gone a week. Mary Noland had high blood pressure and the local doctor had told her to give up pork and other salty food or she would die. Luvenia nursed her as best she could, but Mary wouldn't eat and seemed to be in great pain. Luvenia was worried about her children and finally sent for her mother's sister. With the understanding that her aunt could only stay for one night, Luvenia set off walking back to Belle Parker's in the pouring rain. At home, all the clothes she had washed were off the line and on the ground, driven into the dirt by the torrential rains. Luvenia picked everything up, piled the wet, dirty clothes on the porch, and made her way through the house. She swept out the trash and washed the dishes. When the children came home from school, she washed Julia's and Mae Bertha's hair and found some clean clothes for them. She explained that she had to go back, and when Willie Boyd got off work, he took Luvenia to her mother's in the car.

The house was full of people when Luvenia arrived. It was customary for friends and neighbors to come and sit with the sick, particularly as the end drew near. The following day, unable to bear her mother's suffering, Luvenia did not go into the sick room. She was out on the porch when a neighbor told her that her mother was calling for her.

"Luvenia, give me your hand." Luvenia took her mother's hand but was looking away from her.

"Honey, I want you to promise me one thing. I want you to promise me that you are going to keep your kids until they get grown or until you pass, even if you ain't got nothing but bread and water. Will you promise me that?" Luvenia made the promise, but Mary wouldn't let go of her hand. "I want to look at my child as long as I can," she remembered her mother saying. Luvenia stood there. She finally took her hand away and went back out on the porch. There was a general scurrying in the house and Luvenia knew her mother was dead.

"Has she passed?" Luvenia asked someone.

"Oh no, honey."

"Quit lying to that child," someone else said. "Honey, your mama's gone."

Mary Noland was forty-eight years old. Luvenia told me the story fifty-five years later as if it were yesterday.

ON A Saturday night the following November, Luvenia was at home sewing by the fire. She was pregnant with her first child by Willie Boyd. Leroy, who was four, told her that his head hurt. Luvenia rubbed his head for a while and everyone went to bed. Leroy, Mae Bertha, Julia, and Ida Mae all slept in one bed. C.H. and Jesse slept in another bed in the same room. Luvenia and Willie slept in the living room.

Just after midnight Luvenia heard a peculiar moaning noise coming from the children's room. Leroy came running out and fell onto his mother's bed. He called out, "Come on, Piejo," using his brother Jesse's nickname. Those were his last words. Luvenia put him in her bed and as soon as Willie Boyd got home carried him to the doctor. Dr. B. O. McDaniel in Merigold examined Leroy, who was limp and unresponsive, but couldn't say what the problem was. They took him back home. The next day the doctor came out to the house, but he still couldn't rouse the boy. Little Julia said they had all been picking green peanuts off the bush and that Leroy had eaten them despite her warnings. C.H. said that Leroy had found some old candy in the dump.

On Sunday evening, Luvenia sent for her mother-in-law, Julia, who came to see her grandson one last time. The next day Luvenia touched his face and realized he wasn't breathing. She sat down by the fireplace and called to Julia to look at him. Julia dried her hands and went to the little boy. "Luvenia, he's gone." They buried four-year-old Leroy in the cemetery at Union Grove Church. Luvenia had no burial insurance, so Belle Parker paid for the funeral.

Because Belle Parker's farm required only a small workforce, the four black sharecropping families came to know each other well. Indeed, three of the families were related. Willie Kelly came from Macon, Georgia, to Mississippi in 1907. When he had saved enough money, he sent for his mother, Lucy Scott, and his sisters. Two of the sisters, Annie Moore and Maggie Griffin, also settled at Belle Parker's. Annie Moore and her fifteen-year-old son, K.C., lived a quarter of a mile from Belle Parker's house, and Maggie Griffin lived next door with her son, a twenty-five-year-old man who seemed very responsible and was a good farmer. Belle Parker entrusted him with managing much of the work on her place. His name was Matthew Carter.

Many years later when Luvenia had moved north, leaving Matthew and Mae Bertha, by then married, at Belle Parker's, the older Carter children would visit their great-grandmother Lucy Scott, whom they called Big Gran, to "find out firsthand what happened in the past." She told them stories about the birds—about eagles that would swoop down into fields and about a white man who would take up his gun and kill the great eagles and put them in his wagon, afraid that the birds were stealing his slaves. Lucy Scott had been a slave in Georgia, and later a runaway, and she told her great-grandchildren of the slave quarters, of being fed no better than cattle and swine, of the other slaves—some of whom cooked, some of whom were field hands, and some of whom were used "to bring other slaves into this world—breeders."

Mae Bertha told me that she and her brother C.H. began to make friends with the other families at Belle Parker's. C.H. and fifteen-year-old K.C. Moore, one year older, admired Belle Parker's two-tone, beige-and-chocolate-brown 1928 Model T. Matthew, K.C., and C.H. all became drivers for her, and one or the other of them drove her several times a week into Drew or Cleveland to take care of her errands and business.

Mae Bertha's favorite place to visit was Maggie Griffin's. There she would sit enchanted and watch Matthew and K.C. help Maggie quilt. Suspended from the ceiling, the quilt backing hung down whenever they had time to sew on it. Other times, it was rolled back up to make room for cooking, eating, and sleeping in the two-room cabin. Matthew was fifteen years older than Mae Bertha, but by the time she was fifteen they were courting.

Mae Bertha said that people often told her that she had a mean streak when she was growing up. "Mean," in those circles, was defined as standing up for yourself. Luvenia assured Mae Bertha that people had accused her of the same thing. "You may be mean, Mae Bertha, but you aren't bad."

The years at Belle Parker's were good ones for Luvenia in many ways. Willie Boyd was getting paid twenty-five dollars a month, C.H. plowed for Belle Parker, and Luvenia and her other children worked in cotton, corn, and soybeans to help Belle raise her crops. In addition to sharecropping her own acreage, Luvenia had a vegetable garden, and Belle Parker gave Mae Bertha and Julia clothes and sometimes money for shoes.

The Great Depression was just starting to lift when Luvenia moved to Belle Parker's. She had not known much about President Franklin Roosevelt except that he was a Democrat and that he was supposed to have pulled them out of the Depression. She heard that it was because of Roosevelt that staple foods—sugar and flour—were only five cents a pound. She heard stories of how the president was giving land to poor white farmers just over the river on the Sunflower Plantation.

When outsiders asked to live and work on her place, Belle Parker never considered replacing Luvenia and her kids. Their shack and garden were kept especially for them, but come settlement time each December, when plantation owners subtracted their tenants' expenses from earnings for cotton bales picked, feelings on both sides gave way to economic reality. Liking Luvenia did not keep Belle Parker from underpaying her. Nor did the relationship keep Luvenia from asking Mrs. Parker to "analyze her account" every year when payment was not what Luvenia thought it should be.

In the late thirties, Belle Parker began to have problems with her feet, and a bell on her porch attached to a rope going to her bedroom enabled her to summon Luvenia or Willie Boyd. One morning in early March 1940 she rang for help. K.C. Moore and Willie Boyd rushed her into town to the doctor, but she died on March 18 and was buried in the cemetery at Ruleville. All of the sharecroppers and their families attended the funeral. Belle Parker's last will and testament read: "I will every thing I have to my sister Emma Talley. Land, mules, cow, chickens, wagons, car, mowing machine, rake & all plow tools, household and kitchen furniture."

Emma Talley did not stay on at the Parker place. She moved back to Arkansas with her brother. Except for occasional visits from Judge Parker, Willie Boyd and Matthew Carter took over the total management of the farm, and Luvenia and her family moved into Belle Parker's house.

These years, though better for Luvenia, were hardest for her son C.H. As the oldest, he had conscientiously tried to fill the void his father had left. Growing up as a black male in the Delta, he was acutely aware of the oppressive racism and white sadism. Once when he was seven and visiting his grandmother over on Birch Plantation, C.H. discovered that a white fellow at the Birch commissary was giving black kids candy in exchange for a chance to whip them. The man tried to get C.H. one day, but C.H. told him that he would never be whipped for candy, and he told his playmates that his grandmother had enough money for him to buy whatever candy he wanted. It was true that after Will Noland's death Mary sold one small piece of land and used the money to help her grandchildren in small ways. C.H. was proud of that.

As he grew older, the probability of racial confrontation increased.

Doing odd jobs and daywork meant that C.H. often walked by Millen's Bridge, which connected the roads between Mound Bayou and Drew. A sign was nailed to the bridge: "Nigger, read and run. If you can't read, run anyway."

C.H. married when he was eighteen, worked for a dollar a day on neighboring plantations, and by 1939 had saved enough money to go north to Ohio. Three years later, when Luvenia was forty-two years old, C.H. persuaded her to move to Toledo. He and his wife were living there, and his sister Julia had already joined them. Luvenia's ten-year common-law marriage to Willie Boyd had assured her of food and some security during difficult years, but she wanted to leave Mississippi for good. Luvenia packed the children's clothing in a big trunk she borrowed from a neighbor and packed her clothing in her own trunk and several small suitcases. Another neighbor took the trunks and suitcases to the train depot in Cleveland. Mae Bertha told me that Willie Boyd made no effort to keep Luvenia from leaving and even drove her and the children to town early so that Luvenia and Ida Mae could get their hair done before the trip.

Luvenia arrived in Toledo with the six children in September 1943. About six months later, Willie Boyd went to Toledo and begged Luvenia either to let him move up there with her or to come back with him to Mississippi. She would have none of it. She had waited a long time. Her only regret was leaving one child there—her first daughter, Mae Bertha. By 1943, Mae Bertha was eighteen years old, was married to Matthew Carter, and had three daughters of her own. They remained at Belle Parker's. The seeds were planted.

Part III

The Intolerable Burden

Sign at Drew, Mississippi, city limits, 1971.

*Mae Bertha and Matthew Carter at home
with children, Drew, Mississippi, 1969.*

Seven

She Wouldn't Let Us Say We Wished
We Had Never Been Born

The suit against the Drew school district, brought by Mae Bertha Carter on behalf of her children Larry, Stanley, Gloria, Pearl, Beverly, Deborah, and Carl, was filed in June 1967 in the United States District Court for the Northern District of Mississippi, Greenville Division. Mae Bertha was represented by the NAACP Legal Defense and Educational Fund lawyer Marian Wright (later Marian Wright Edelman); Paul and Iris Brest and Reuben Anderson, three lawyers working with Wright in Jackson, Mississippi; and Jack Greenberg, the director of the Defense Fund. It was a class-action suit, and it described the shooting, eviction, and general harassment related to the Carters' desegregation efforts. "Fear of white retaliation," it stated, "firmly grounded in fact, has deterred other Negroes from choosing the formerly white schools pursuant to the district's freedom of choice plan."

The suit claimed that two years after the freedom of choice plan was implemented, Matthew and Mae Bertha Carter's children remained the only black children in Drew's previously all-white schools. It named as defendants the superintendent of education, the five members of the board of trustees, and "their agents, employees, successors, and all those in active concert with them." It carefully outlined the school system's continuing failure to hire black personnel at the white schools; the segregated school buses; and nine alleged instances of superior programs and facilities at schools that still had white students only but that continued to receive federal funds. The suit asked for injunctive relief against the operation of a racially segregated and discriminatory system that placed a "cruel and intolerable burden" on black parents and pupils, and called the whole system a violation of the Fourteenth Amendment. But by its very nature the seven-page document could not come close to evoking the true nature of the "intolerable burden" borne by the Carter children beginning on that first day of school in 1965.

A GAP of four years separated what Mae Bertha calls her first and second batches of children. Ruth, born on May 14, 1949, was the oldest of the second batch of eight children, but she had felt the discontent of her five older sisters and brothers and had watched them leave home, one by one. When Ruth and I first met in 1966, I sensed her deep anger. She was quiet, often withdrawn, but as she remembered the terror of Emmett Till's murder and the harassment of blacks after the Supreme Court's *Brown* decision, she began to seethe.

In February 1990, twenty years after the last time I'd seen her, I went to Toledo, Ohio, to talk to Ruth again about what it was like to lead the way in the family's 1965 decision to change schools. I noticed that she had retained the stubborn seriousness I remembered, and I couldn't help thinking of something Mae Bertha once told me: "You know, I had to spank Ruth when she was little," Mae Bertha had said. "She just wouldn't pick cotton. I'd come out in the fields and she would just be standing there like she was looking at the birds and the trees. We needed that cotton money to feed our family. And then, when she *would* pick, she would only use one hand, rather than two like she was supposed to."

Ruth left Mississippi for good in 1970 and moved in with her older sister Bertha in Toledo. She took care of Bertha's children until she married a year later. For twenty years she has worked as a teacher's aide for handicapped kindergarten children in the Toledo public school system. Today she is divorced and lives with her two teenage daughters, Ngina and Tandra.

After picking me up at the Toledo airport, Ruth drove first to her grandmother Luvenia's house, where I made an appointment to interview her. Then we went on to Ruth's apartment where I met her two daughters. Ngina, who was then fifteen, left for work, but nine-year-old Tandra sat with us in the living room to hear her mother's story.

"What I hated the most was being in the cotton field and seeing the white school buses pass us by while we were picking," Ruth said.

"They'd always have new buses, and when we finally started to school, we would get their leftover buses just like the leftover school-books. On the side of the books it would say 'Race—White,' and they had been handed down to us. I never thought any of it was right, and I always thought Mississippi was a terrible place to live and a terrible way to live, and I always dreamed of the day that I would be able to leave.

"In August of 1965, when the freedom of choice papers came, I was the oldest at home and entering the eleventh grade. At first I thought, I don't know—all my friends and everything are at the black school and I don't know whether I want to leave them. But my older sister Naomi was there, and she said to me, 'Ruth, if you sign that paper to go to the all-white school, maybe, just maybe, you won't have to go to the cotton field.' And I laughed and said, 'Yeah.'

"So we really jumped at the chance to integrate the school because at least we could get away from the cotton fields, and because we thought it would, you know, later on, make the world a better place. We knew it was the right thing to do.

"So we all decided that we wanted to go—from me the oldest to Deborah the youngest—but the little ones really didn't know what they were doing. Larry, Stanley, and I signed our own papers, but Mama came home from St. Louis and signed the ones for the rest of the kids. She took the papers back to the school and that's how we enrolled.

"I didn't think we were going to be the only ones—my friend Nettie who'd been to jail with me, I thought she was going, too. But something happened—I think her parents changed their minds, and she wasn't there in September.

"After we started to school, because I was the oldest, I thought maybe the younger kids were looking up to me and that I was there to protect them if something happened—if something went wrong. This affected my life in a way. I am a nervous person anyway—and any black person who lived in Mississippi at that time should understand how afraid we were—well, it just affected me. We had to ride the school bus with all those white kids and they would throw spitballs and call us all kinds of names, and I'm sitting there and can't do a thing. And there's my little sisters and brothers, and Deborah, only six years old and so sweet and precious to me, being mistreated, and there was nothing I could do. I got so depressed. It seemed like I just filled up with hatred from my toes to the top of my head. I didn't think I was going to be able to handle it.

"And then there was the bus. We were the first to get on in the morning, and the first day we just sat near the front of the bus, and the other kids got on and sat behind us. This happened for a while, and then one day the bus driver said, 'Go to the back of the bus.' So we went, and I think it was on a Friday, because Stanley told us over the weekend, 'I'm not going to the back on Monday.' So he sat in the front and the bus driver looked at him and said, 'I shouldn't have to tell you what to do—get to the back.'

"The next day at school, the assistant superintendent called us all together. They had gone over to A. W. James Elementary School and picked up Deborah, Pearl, and Beverly. They came and got me in gym class and we all went to the superintendent's office. He asked us what was going on with the bus and we told him about having to go to the back. He said he didn't know, and I told him that his assistant knew because he watched the bus load in the afternoon and had seen us walk to the back. Then he dismissed us and said the bus would stop first at A. W. James that afternoon and then would come to the high school. So when the bell rang at 3:00, we went out to the bus, and Pearl, Deborah, and Beverly were sitting there in the front, and we sat next to them. When we got home, Deborah told us that she went to the back of the bus when she first got on, but the driver sent a little white kid to tell her to come back to the front. So after that we always rode up front. That bus driver had driven the bus for something like eighteen years and the next year he gave up his job. I think people kept pressuring him to make us sit in the back. Things like that always upset me. I always felt responsible for anything that went wrong.

"I don't think my sisters and brothers ever thought about pulling out. I know I didn't, and if they did, I didn't know about it. Thinking about pulling out—it was like being a loser—you start something, you finish it. During that time, it seemed like I was filled up with hate. I hated Mississippi. I hated the white man. I hated my teachers. I hated everything. Then we started having these little sessions at home in the afternoon after school. It was almost like therapy. We would sit down and Mama would say, 'How did things go today at school?' We would talk about what happened and a lot of times we would cry together. After we'd talk and sit down and cry together, things would seem a little better.

"If Mama heard me say, 'I hate white people, I just can't stand them,' she always answered, 'Don't you ever say that. Don't you ever say that you hate white people or anyone—it's not right.'

"And I answered, 'How would you know, Mama? We're the ones who have to stay in school with them all day. We have to ride the bus with them and go to the lunchroom with them where they won't sit next to us. We're the ones they throw spitballs at and call 'nigger.'

"But she got on us every time we said we hated them. The other thing she wouldn't let us say was that we wished we had never been born.

"Gloria had study period right before lunch, so she could leave and go to the lunchroom early and there would be plenty of places for her to sit alone. But Larry and Stanley and I had to go with the rest of the school, and there weren't many places to sit, and when we'd sit beside a white person they would jump a mile away. So we decided that the three of us wouldn't eat lunch and we saved the quarters that Mama gave us for lunch money each morning. Stanley put his in a little can and hid it on top of the house, but one day Daddy found the can, and that night he and Mama called all of us in and asked where the quarters had come from—had we been eating our lunches? Gloria was the only one eating. They made us promise to eat, and we did for a couple of days, but the white kids still jumped away like we were poison and it hurt us. So one day I thought, I will buy my lunch like I promised, but I'm not going to eat. I went and got the lunch and gave them the quarter, then took the lunch, dumped it in the wastebasket, and went on outside.

"We all stopped eating lunch again for a long time, and then the janitor who worked at the school told Daddy. After that we took our lunch to school and ate on the steps.

"But after I got older and was on my own, I came to Toledo and started going to a Lutheran church, and I had a white pastor. I guess my feelings toward white people changed, and then I would think, well Mama was right about hate, because you don't feel good about yourself when you hate someone else."

Ruth, her two daughters, and I went out to lunch. On the way back to her apartment, Ruth asked me if I knew the name Archie Manning; he was a white classmate of hers at Drew High School. I did—he had been a famous football quarterback at the University of Mississippi who later played for the New Orleans Saints. When we got home she showed me the June 8, 1981, issue of *Sports Illustrated*, which featured an article about Archie Manning entitled "The Patience of a Saint." The article spoke of his part in Mississippi history when "integration" came to Drew and "seven jittery children from a family named Carter" broke the color line. Manning was quoted as remembering that "it was a very tense situation, but you can't change the place you grew up in or the way you grew up."

The article also quoted Ruby Nell Stancill, a white math teacher at the high school. "There was no violence," she said, "no ugly incidents that made headlines. The people here aren't like that. The Carter children were simply ignored." Ruth Carter's letter to *Sports Illustrated* appeared in the June 29 issue:

> Sir:
>
> There are a couple of things I'd like to say about writer Paul Zimmerman's description of the time when integration came to Drew High. It would be very interesting to know what Ruby Nell Stancill meant. . . . I think the article should have said that the Carter children simply ignored the rest of the students. Ignored spitballs, name calling and other little nasty remarks. If you had wanted to know why the Carter children ate on the gym steps

instead of in the cafeteria, I could have told you; but the article, of course, was about Archie Manning. I could write a book about Drew, Miss. and how it "isn't redneck country."

Ruth Carter Whittle
Toledo, Ohio

"Archie Manning was one of those who didn't say anything to me at all," Ruth told me. "Then something strange happened. I was upset about a history teacher talking about nigger this and nigger that. But late in October that first year, I was sitting in class and someone tapped me on my shoulder and handed me this letter—this note. I read it and then I folded it up and brought it home. It was printed and read: 'DEAR RUTH, WE ARE ALL VERY MUCH IN SYMPATHY WITH YOU. WE HATE THE WAY SOME PEOPLE HAVE BEEN TREATING YOU. WE ALL LOVE YOU VERY MUCH. LOVE, JOHNNY STACY, GEORGE HATCHER, PHIL SHURDEN, PHILLOR MORRIS, JOE SKEEN, ROBERT MOODY.' All of the signers' names were in the same large print. I never knew who gave me the note and none of the signers ever approached me or showed a different attitude from the other white children. I didn't know what to think—it was all from only boys."

In 1991, when I was back in Drew interviewing people, I saw Johnny Stacy Baughman and asked him about the note. He told me it was probably a joke played by another—unnamed—student on the six white boys whose names were on the letter.

Ruth continued, "None of the girls in the class ever tried to be friends with me. There was one girl that would always speak if she saw me before school or after school; she would say, 'Hi,' and smile, and that was it. But she would never say anything to me in front of her friends. Then one girl my senior year asked me for a picture, so I gave her one.

"I didn't do too well at studying. I couldn't do it—I was so full of hatred, and I couldn't relax enough to study. At the all-black school I had pretty good grades, but then my grades began to fall. My outlook, my attitude, my feelings toward the people that surrounded me—it hurt a lot and there was a difference in my grades when I changed schools.

"And things weren't any better my senior year. The hardest thing was finding out I had to go back for another year and take two subjects over. I cried and cried when I found out I had to go back. They had let me buy my class ring, send out invitations, and get my cap and gown. I was so hurt. And the next year, 1968, was pretty much the same. I can remember that was the year Dr. King was assassinated. When I walked into school that morning, the other kids were laughing and it seemed to be aimed toward me. That was a sad year. Things didn't really get any better until the school was completely integrated.

"But I'm not sorry about the decision to go to the all-white school. That's one thing in life I'm not sorry about! I would do it over again. I think my mom was fed up with Mississippi and the life that she was living. She knew there should be something better for her and her family. And it was probably the sixties when everybody was fighting for their rights, and blacks were tired of the white-only signs and the white-only life, and the civil rights mass meetings and the singing of the songs helped push things along. I know they did for me.

"Now my dad, he was just always there for us. He didn't talk or speak much about it, but we knew that we could count on him and he agreed with the things we believed—the things we wanted—he wanted them too, but being a man . . . Mississippi was kind of hard on black men, and I think the women did more of the pushing for rights in the South, but he was always there for us. See, black men were subjected to so much—the brutality and violence—if they stepped out of line. He was a beautiful person, a swell daddy, we just loved him—we said it all in the eulogy at his funeral and we meant it. We loved him and he loved us—it was all the love in our family that held us together in the bad times.

"I would like to write a book about my life, starting from six years old and about my dreams—some of them have come true, you know. At least I got out of the cotton fields, so I guess dreams can come true."

At the end of Ruth's story, I asked Tandra if she had heard any of this before. She shook her head. It was the first time. Then Tandra looked at Ruth and said, "I think *my* mother's a Wonder Woman."

LARRY, NEXT in line after Ruth, was born in 1950. He joined the air force in 1972 and served for twenty years. In 1991, his wife, Chong Suk, whom he met in Korea, his daughter, Shawnee, and son, Darren, came to stay with Mae Bertha for six months because Larry might be sent to the Gulf War. (Mae Bertha told me later that she had become a real convert to Chong Suk's Korean cooking.) I met Larry and his family in Philadelphia, Pennsylvania, in June 1991, when they were returning to the base in Turkey where he was stationed.

Larry recalled that by the time he was fifteen, and Ruth was sixteen, they had already made up their minds about going to the white school and that signing the freedom of choice forms was just the final step: "I don't remember being afraid when I went to the tenth grade at the white school—just a little apprehensive. We were changing classes by then, and I was worried about finding rooms and places in a new school. The thing I remember the most is learning math from my math teacher, Ruby Nell Stancill. Math was my favorite subject and I did pretty good in it. And the librarian was nice. She would help me find books and sometimes she would go to a shelf and say, 'You'd probably like this—it's a good book.' But I hated history class when we covered the Civil War and the teacher said 'nigger' and allowed the students to say it like I wasn't even there.

"None of the white students ever associated with us and we weren't involved in any activities. Basically we just went to school there. But there was one student who bothered me and I don't know why. We had to go upstairs and downstairs to class and when I went downstairs he'd be waiting for me and would come up behind me. I'd have my books under my arm and he'd kick his knee up and knock the books down. So I finally started waiting for him until we could walk down the steps side by side. He was a year behind me, and my senior year we got to leave things to juniors—see, I had this patch of gray hair on the back of my head—I donated that patch of gray hair to him. They read it at the last assembly and everybody broke up laughing.

"And I remember when we quit eating in the cafeteria. We'd be sitting all alone at this big long table and everybody would be looking at us. See, at the black school, we didn't have glasses for our milk. We'd just open the carton and drink. And at the white school they had straws or glasses, and we weren't familiar with that. For them, drinking from a carton was a big thing, and they stared at us—at how we drank our milk and ate our food.

"Once toward the end of the first semester, we were in the field picking cotton after school and I told Mama that I was going back to the other school. Then we had a discussion. She told me about how she and Daddy had committed themselves to the choice and how

Daddy had sacrificed so many things so we could go and how I should try and stick it out. She never did say I couldn't change schools, she just explained things to me. That was the last time I ever thought about leaving—that conversation in the cotton field took about thirty minutes.

"Things didn't change much in the tenth, eleventh, or twelfth grades. I just separated school from my personal life. I went to school, studied, 3:15 came, school was out, I did my homework and chores, and I had black friends at the other school, and we went to football games and events there. Then Ruth had to make up some courses, so she and I graduated together in 1968. All the family came, but I don't remember any particular emotions except that it was graduation day. But my father put his arm around me and walked with me after graduation and told me how proud he was of me."

Larry retired from the air force in 1994. While in the air force, he earned a master's degree in public administration. He now lives with his family in Hampton, Virginia.

I MADE my first visit back to Mississippi in 1989, after my reunion with Mae Bertha in Atlanta the previous fall. Several of her children were visiting her while I was there. One was Stanley, who had driven up from Longview, Texas, where he lives with his wife, Carrie Mae, and their son, Stanley, Jr. Born in 1952, Stanley was next in the line of children, following Ruth and Larry. He entered the eighth grade at Drew High School in 1965.

"Now basically from the eighth grade through graduation, it was the same at the school," Stanley recalled. "I was with the same classmates and they didn't change any. The atmosphere was just as bad when I finished as when I started. At graduation, I still had some white kids up there kicking my heels in line, throwing spitballs. You spend five years with them and they're still throwing spitballs at graduation. So we didn't change their attitude—they were set in their ways. I mean you could tell some of the kids were decent, but when you're that age, you got to act like your peers—you have to pretend you're like them. But you can look through a person and tell what type of person he is. They all acted up because they were showing off for their peers even though it may not have been in their hearts. But I think the boys were worst. The girls didn't have too much to say.

"Of course I didn't understand all that back then, and plenty of times I thought I was going to tell my parents that I wasn't going back. I think the first year was the worst. It would be so bad—you'd be sitting there and you'd hate for the next day to come, because you knew you got to go back into that school and put up with all that harassment all over again. Then I got sort of used to it. You sort of put it in the back of your mind and say, 'Well, I am here for just one reason.' And then it became a routine. You go to school, you get harassed—you know it's going to be there. You just put on blinders.

"The main thing about it, you knew after the first year, they were trying to get you out of the school, so you couldn't let them defeat you. See, so you had to stick it out, 'cause you didn't want them to feel like they had won. So then all that stuff they had done to you—when they thought you'd get so disgusted you'd leave—you'd have taken it all for nothing and they'd have won. So it was sort of like a contest, between, you know, us and them."

DEBORAH CARTER Smith was also visiting her mother in Drew that June weekend. Deborah and her sister Pearl live about eighty miles from Drew, in Oxford, home of the University of Mississippi. Deborah is the twelfth Carter child, born on Busyline in 1959. She works in the accounting department at the university, is married to James E. Smith, and has two sons, James, Jr., and Jarryl. The Carters had moved from Busyline into Drew before Deborah was old enough to go into the cotton fields, so she was spared picking and chopping. She was the youngest of the seven children who entered the white schools in 1965. I asked her what she could remember about it.

"I integrated A. W. James grammar school as a first-grader, but I don't remember the first day at all. I remember being there after a while and that my first-grade teacher was nice to me. And the other kids were only five and six so I really didn't have any hassle. But I do remember one time when we had to walk over to the high school. They were having a circus and kids from kindergarten and first grade had to walk the two or three blocks and each student had to have a partner. And I do remember that I had to hold hands and walk with the teacher, but I just thought that it was great because I got to walk with the teacher.

"In the second grade, when Beverly had to move over to the other side of the school where the fourth through sixth grades were held, I was by myself. I remember not having any playmates and that this one white girl played with me until the principal called her in and told her not to be playing with me and that then I had to play by myself again. It was always harder around recess.

"I remember liking English a lot in school—learning how to say your consonant sounds and vowels. In the third grade, they taught us how to talk on the telephone, and since we had moved into Drew and finally had one, it was fun to learn how to talk on it. When I was in the fourth grade, a black school teacher sent her son. We were in the same class, so then there were two of us, and I can remember being happy that he was there. Then, in the fifth grade, actual integration came."

DURING MY visit, after Stanley and Deborah had left for their homes, I had a chance to talk to Beverly Carter, the only Carter child who has remained in Drew. Beverly was born in 1957. She and her two children, Kerry and Shayla, have a house in Drew, but they spend most of their time at Mae Bertha's. I have always been impressed that Mae Bertha, after raising thirteen children, still wants them home whenever possible and is happiest when surrounded by her grandchildren. I asked Beverly about being a third-grader at A. W. James Elementary School.

"How I hated recesses. None of the other children would play with us, so we would go and stand out beside the wall or sit on the steps. Once after lunch, white children were playing on those steps, and I guess they did it to be mean, and I didn't know where to go. I was just standing there until the principal—I guess she was nice—came out and asked the kids to leave so we could sit there.

"I wanted to say to Mama, 'I want to go where people will play with me, or, you know, like me.' But I never did. White kids would come by and call me names, from 'nigger' to 'walking Tootsie Roll.' God, I wanted to cry, to disappear, to go home. I never cried, at least not until I was older . . . when I was in the fifth grade I did. We had just moved into the city limits of Drew and now I had a chance to meet some black children my own age. Somehow they could not understand why I was going to an all-white school. They said that I thought

I was white . . . that hurt more than any of the bad names the white kids had called me—and I cried.

"And I think it might have gotten worse as I got older, because in junior high, like when I was in the seventh grade, the white children would still push you and kick you and throw things at you."

WHEN I was in Mississippi a second time in 1989 to visit Mae Bertha, Pearl drove over from Oxford. Pearl is the office manager for the Mid-Valley Pipeline Company there. She is divorced and lives with her two children, Latoya and Jason. Pearl, who was born in 1955, entered the fifth grade at A. W. James the first year of the Carters' integration. She had a much worse experience than her sisters and brothers. When I asked her about it, she replied, "How can I describe it? Five years of hell? I remember people being mean to me the whole five years until full integration came in the tenth grade, but the first year was the worst, because I just happened to get a teacher who was really cruel to me. I remember her asking me questions like where had I gotten my glasses—from the NAACP? The teachers with my brothers and sisters just kind of went along with what was going on, but this teacher I had was furious and she really mistreated me.

"They always said we had an odor, so my father used to get up every morning and would run that bath water and get that soap and deodorant and that perfume and make sure our clothes were clean and he would just rub and scrub us down because he just wanted to make sure that they were just lying. And when I'd get to school, the teacher wouldn't let any white child sit by me more than a week, and every week she would move the child in front of me and behind . . . she would take them out in the hall . . . she would have a talk with them. I guess she just kept a list, 'cause you knew some of them had to come back around before the year was ended. It was just awful, and even when these kids would sit by me, they would pull their chair up and away and the ones behind would push theirs back, so I was kind of sitting there by myself. I had to go through that a whole year.

"I told my mother and she contacted someone who came to the school and talked to the principal and he talked with my teacher. And the teacher stopped like a week or two and then she started all over again. She hurt me deep down inside.

"Now there was one white girl that never did anything ugly to me the whole time, but she was the only one—actually she had brothers and sisters, so it was a family, but she was the only one in the classroom with me. She didn't really talk to me, but she never jumped out of the way when I passed right by her, while the other kids always pretended like we had an odor or that our color would rub off on them or something, and if we got close to them they would just jump, but this one girl didn't. She was a nice girl.

"I don't know whether it's because when you are young it doesn't hurt as bad. I don't know *what* it was, but I don't ever remember telling Mother, 'I just give up, I just don't want to do this anymore.' I feel like if I had to do it now, I couldn't at this age. But at that age I wanted to continue something that I started, and I did understand a little. Mother was talking to us a lot, and I knew I didn't have an odor. I knew they had to be mean to show us they didn't want us there, and I kept thinking, 'I deserve to be here just like you.' That's the one thing Mama always preached. One time we said something about the white school, and she said, 'That school is not white, it's brown brick, and that school belongs to you as well as it belongs to them—always remember that.'"

GLORIA CARTER Dickerson, the ninth of the thirteen Carter children, now lives in Jackson. After Pearl left to go back home to Oxford, Mae Bertha decided to ride with my sister Ann and me to visit Gloria for a while. The fields were heavy with lush, green plants. I had looked at a lot of cotton in the 1960s, but I still had to ask Mae Bertha to identify the different crops. She pointed out the fields of soybeans, rice, and cotton. My sister asked Mae Bertha what she thought when she looked at those long rows of cotton. "Look," Mae Bertha said, "I wouldn't care if I never saw another cotton plant as long as I live."

Gloria lives with her son, Deidrick, in a large ranch-style house in a Jackson suburb. Her husband, Donald, works for the Tennessee Valley Authority in Memphis and commutes to Jackson on weekends. Gloria fixed dinner for us. She told us that this was a rarity, because she doesn't like to cook. Her job as vice-president of finance for MINACT, which provides education and vocational training to disadvantaged youths, is demanding and requires out-of-town travel two or three times a month. Gloria attended night classes and received an M.B.A. from Millsaps College in Jackson in 1992.

Gloria was born in 1953. She entered the seventh grade at Drew High School and remembers no time when she was close to quitting: "In 1965, it was really Ruth who wanted to go to the school. Or maybe Larry too—anyway, it was the older ones. But mostly I remember Ruth saying she wanted to go. I followed and said, 'Okay, I want to go too.' And I got very excited—so excited I just couldn't wait. I thought it was going to be a lot different. I wanted to go because I thought, this is going to be a better school, the building nicer, the buses cleaner. I thought everything was going to be nicer. I was ready. I wanted to go. Was I in for a disappointment!

"It just hurt. I'd go home after school and pray about it and say, 'Dear Lord, don't let this happen tomorrow—let tomorrow be an okay day. Don't let anybody hit me with a spitball.' Some days you'd get by without a spitball hitting you upside the head, but not many, not many at all. Mostly every day someone would say, 'That nigger did this,' or, 'This nigger don't know that.' It was like an everyday thing, but it's something you never got used to. It's not like the seventh grade was okay and by the eighth you adjusted so you didn't mind. You *never* got used to it.

"But we never once thought of quitting. I kept saying, 'I can't quit. They can't make me leave. We are not going to lose—we are not going to let 'em run us away.'

"When I was at the black school, I was a straight-A student all the way through the sixth grade. The seventh grade was different and it was hard. The first part of the year, my grades dropped, probably to Bs and Cs. I never got any Ds or Fs, but in the beginning I had to adjust and my grades did drop. But by the eighth grade they went back up to where they had always been and from the ninth through twelfth it wasn't hard anymore—I only got one B and it was in biology. Probably at first my study habits weren't like they should have been, but I realized it pretty soon and started studying more.

"I had some pretty nice teachers—most of them were nice as far as instruction. They didn't go out of their way to be friendly or anything like that, but if I had a question I always felt at ease about asking in class and I did. They would always answer the question. Now, none of them ever stopped the white students from saying or doing things to us, and they weren't friendly to us, but they did respond to my questions, so that was the good thing about it. And I had Ruby Nell Stancill in math the ninth through twelfth and she was good. I mean, she gave me lots of attention if I wanted it, if I had a question. She was an excellent teacher, and she was fair and she would explain. She would stop right then and explain things just like she would do any of the other kids. So she treated me like anyone else in terms of the material. She was neutral on being sociable, but of all my teachers in school, she sticks out as the most fair teacher.

"I was really surprised that there were no other blacks there, 'cause I really thought there would be and looked for them when I first got there. I couldn't believe we were the only ones who had decided to go. I kept looking for some of my classmates from the sixth grade. You know we didn't have a telephone so we couldn't communicate over the summer, but I looked for some of my friends on the first day of school, surely *somebody* else had chosen to go. Anybody ought to want a better or cleaner school. I just wasn't aware of the racism or the problems it was going to cause. I didn't know enough to be aware that we weren't supposed to be doing this—like we were told to choose our schools but weren't really supposed to do it. I thought you just decided with no bad effects or anything like that. I thought the choice was normal.

"You know, up until a few years ago, I was still having nightmares about being in Drew High School, and I would wake up sobbing."

CARL, THE youngest of the thirteen Carter children, was born January 5, 1961, at Pembles' Plantation on Busyline. Since the family moved to Drew in 1966 when he was five, like Deborah, he never had to pick cotton. His only memory of the fateful choice is the school bus stopping in front of the house on Busyline and his wishing he could get on with his brothers and sisters. When he entered the first grade in 1967, he and Deborah were the only two black students in the A. W. James Elementary School.

I talked to Carl in May 1990 in Drew when he had driven over from his home in Columbus, Mississippi, to see Mae Bertha for Mother's Day. He and his wife, Upea, have a daughter, Kutee, and a son, Bryan. Carl is the assistant director of materials management at Baptist Memorial Hospital–Golden Triangle. I had not seen him since he was fourteen.

"It was kind of unusual to go to school with white kids and then come back home and play only with black kids. And even some of them wouldn't play with me, because I went to the 'other school.' My first-grade teacher, Miss Hardy, was nice. I was real quiet and I made good grades, especially in math. I never really played with the white kids at school, but I did have one white friend named Tony Burchfield. I used to just stand up against the wall at recess while the guys were racing. Tony was very fast. He just asked me to run one time and I was kind of fast too and I used to win most of the races and we became friends. There were a lot of Burchfields at school—like three cousins. I played with Tony for the first two years and then the school integrated fully in fall of 1969.

"In the second grade, Deborah went over to the other side of the elementary school and this not having many playmates at home *or* at school made me feel bad, and I ran away from school. I just left the schoolyard one day and came home. I was only seven and I had walked all the way to school in the morning and then I walked all the way home. I told Mama that I had walked all the way home and I wasn't going back. I said I was sick, got in bed, and said I didn't want to go back to school. I remember I just got so tired, and I believe that affected me right to this day. I was already quiet, but I think I became more quiet. Not having any friends just affected me.

"But Mother explained things to me. 'Carl, you just got to go to school. It's in your best interest—you just stay and things will get better.' So I hung in there and then the school became integrated. When the court order came down and all the black kids came, I was in the third grade and it was fine. But those first two years, well, with Deborah gone—couldn't play with her, couldn't even see her—it was rough. I was the only black boy there.

"Now I didn't have any problems much with the studying. Especially in math, when we did the little flashcards and stuff like that, I was real good. I could compete and I got good grades. By the time I got to the twelfth grade, there were a lot of blacks there. In fact, from the fourth grade on, I went to games and activities. I was still a quiet person. But I think maybe I was probably going to be quiet anyway. For me, the worst thing was not having playmates and the sad thing is that when kids are small they do what their parents tell them. So, if the parents said, 'Don't play with this guy,' then they didn't. But all in all, I certainly didn't have the hardships that my sisters and brothers went through."

AS I talked with the Carter children about their experiences, Ruby Nell Stancill, the math teacher at Drew High School, emerged as a major influence in their education and career choices. As Larry told his mother, "Mama, if you don't get math from Ruby Nell Stancill, you just never will."

Ruby Nell Stancill came to Drew from the Mississippi hill country.

She started teaching there in 1951 at an annual salary of two thousand dollars. She taught math to all the Carter children except Ruth, and every one of them voiced respect for her total dedication to teaching them math and for always being fair. When I interviewed Mrs. Stancill and told her about the Carter children's feelings, she was surprised: "I didn't know they felt that way. Each one was just another child in my room and I treated them just exactly as I did the other children. I regret to say that I did not go out of my way to be special to them, and I did not associate with them outside of school. If I saw them uptown, I probably never even spoke to them. They came to school and went home. But if anything did make me different—it's like I tell my children today—'I may not like you and you may not like me, but you're going to be treated fairly and you're going to learn math.'"

Mrs. Stancill was also surprised when I told her about the harassment the Carter children experienced at school. "I always had control of my classroom," she told me. "I seated the children alphabetically and never moved anybody unless they couldn't see and needed a front seat. The Carter children came in on time and took their place, and without exception they never took their eyes off of me during class and that's the way it's supposed to be. I like a relaxed room but I want it controlled. So there were no ugly comments in my room. If they were isolated or ostracized it was unbeknownst to me. It was just a new way of life, and I think that we fear the unknown. We had our little boat that was going along and integration rocked that boat. It was frightening to the white people and to blacks because what we had been accustomed to was changed—two separate ways for all these years and then everything changed—just ruined—is the way most of us felt.

"Then in 1970 when the black and white schools were totally merged, we were really afraid. We didn't know what was going to happen, and it was easy, especially for the Delta people with money, to start the private academies. The white children all went to them—wholesale.

"But through the years, feelings and attitudes relaxed and the two youngest of the children, Carl and Deborah, and I became good friends and now I have a good relationship with all the family. I taught those seven children. Six of them are business or accounting graduates of the University of Mississippi. I feel both humble and proud when their mother walks up to me in public, puts her arms around me, and says, 'My children are where they are today because of you.'"

*Letter from Deborah Carter, in first grade, to AFSC staff
member Jean Fairfax, December 1965.*

Eight

Down Here Is the Lion's Den

During the first weeks of school, Jean Fairfax of the American Friends Service Committee followed up on Prathia Hall Wynn's initial reports and phone calls about the Carter family. Fairfax asked the Boulder Friends Meeting in Colorado to send clothes for the seven school-age children and $8.75 a week to pay for their lunches at school. Fairfax continued to send weekly checks to the Carters from the AFSC office and letters of encouragement with suggestions for ways to cope with the problems at school. Marie Turner of the AFSC's Philadelphia office also began sending clothes for each child from the AFSC clothing warehouse, and she wrote Mae Bertha regularly as both an AFSC staff member and a friend.

The letters of September 1965 from Mae Bertha to the Philadelphia AFSC staff are heartbreaking:

My ten year old girl need eye glasses. She can't see the board in school. More talk that we may have to move at the end of the year. The boss called all the people in and ask what all they know about us and why they hadn't told him. He also said he was going to help the ones that wasn't in the mess. So you can see why I was glad to get the money.

The following week Mae Bertha wrote:

I am writing to let you know about the glasses for Pearl and being qualify for free lunches. I called the superintendent and he said only the people on welfare could have free lunches and I couldn't get glasses through the school. He got real nasty when I ask him about it and hung up the phone. I really believe that Drew need some more Negro children in that school. I don't think they should be receiving all that money with my few little children in there. The school suppose to have been integrated on freedom of choice. A lot of other children could have gone but their parent were afraid of the pressure and someone may shoot in their home just as they did ours. They attitude will probably change since they see my children going on.

Mae Bertha's letters about the hardships she was facing that first year continued into the fall:

Yes I have taken Pearl to the eye doctor. She have bad eyes. The test and glasses $40. I paid $15 down and start Nov. 1, $5.00 a month. We been talking about a place to stay if we do have to move, but we don't know where yet. The people here so mean. We wish we could get a place in Drew but most the Negro people afraid to let us have a place, but we going to try. We need help bad because the boss only let us have $8 when we pick a bale, and we can't pick too much with the kids in school, we have to pick four bales, so that all the cash we had. It hard for the poor to stand up for what is right here. It rains now so no one can pick any cotton. I don't know what we going to do. It is so. But I am sure the Lord will take care of us. I try to tell fact. Don't many people know about Mississippi but the ones been here or live here. The whites here are out to get you, like no place to stay, no food, no job. And this will stop the other Negroes.

I bath my children everyday and put them in clean clothes. When my little ten-year old Pearl get to school she (teacher) tell her to take a bath and put on clean clothes. I think it need somebody to come to that school and investigate. I think the teacher is cracking up. I cannot report it to the principal because he just as mean as the teacher. All of the people out there in Drew is mean."

In late October Mae Bertha wrote:

It is raining here right now. I am so tired from picking cotton. I guess I need some rest. They don't seem to smell Pearl at school anymore. What worry me so much is here on the farm the other children have to miss out of school to pick cotton. Children of eight year and younger. Their school bus be empty. Nobody doing anything about it. I go to mass meeting and the bossman found out and he was shocked. He still want slavery on the farm, because that where all the slavery is.

I am thinking about you all. How the Lord have sent you all into our home and I just want to write you. The superintendent call all the kids in to see what was happening to them. My kids are smart. They did it well. Gloria told about the bus driver saying to go on to the back after Stanley start to sit in front. My kids riding up front now. One day Pearl cried when I gave her lunch money. "Mother don't make me eat there." She told me how the kids treat her, how she left her food. I wrote the teacher. She took it to the principal. I wrote: "Dear teacher: Pearl found it hard to eat because the kids come up and put their fist in her face. Thank you."

The principal told Pearl to tell her mother, don't write no letter and send it out there. So yesterday, the superintendent ask why they wasn't eating. Pearl told him. I hope he do something about it. Deborah's teacher told her to eat and stayed there until she eat. So you see it some good people.

Oh, yes, I am glad to know Miss Marie Turner [at the AFSC] is white. It make me know some day we will all be free. Not all white is mean. We have white friend. I wish she could come to see us. But this is Mississippi, down here is the lion's den. That why we got to stand up for freedom. Nobody got anything to do with who comes to your house. I think it going to be better at the school. At least I hope so.

By Thanksgiving, Jean Fairfax was so worried that she went to visit the Carters over the holidays. The plan was for Jean to fly into Memphis, rent a car, and drive down Highway 61 to Merigold. Matthew was to be sitting on the cab of his truck at a designated service station. He would guide Fairfax back to their house on Busyline. What she discovered in Mississippi was that efforts to run the Carters off the land had escalated. When the cotton was ready, the overseer had put a mechanical cotton-picker in the Carters' fields and then had plowed the plants under, leaving nothing at all for hand-pickers; he told Matthew that it was because he needed the land to plant a cover crop. Clearly the Carters would soon need another place to live, so Fairfax contacted Amzie Moore in Cleveland and Marian Wright at the NAACP Legal Defense and Educational Fund office in Jackson.

Even with no money from the cotton crop, the Carters were able to survive November and December. Amzie Moore brought food, the Boulder Friends continued to send lunch money, the AFSC sent small grants, the Morningside Gardens Civil Rights Committee in New York City contributed clothing and money, and some canned foods came from a church in New Jersey. When the overseer failed to bring the Carters the usual fifteen dollars for their car's annual license plate, Fannie Lou Hamer, by then a leader in the Mississippi Freedom Democratic party, brought Mae Bertha the tag money.

Amzie Moore also contacted Reverend Maurice McCrackin, a white minister who headed Operation Freedom, based in Cincinnati, Ohio. Operation Freedom had started in early 1961 to help black families in western Tennessee after they had been evicted for trying to register to vote. The group had expanded to other states as reprisals increased with the growing freedom movement. McCrackin visited the Carters as soon as he heard about them, and the records of Operation Freedom show that the organization sent the Carters grants when times were hardest. McCrackin corresponded with Mae Bertha and he visited the family two or three times a year. He once told me his favorite quotation from Mae Bertha, on life in Drew: "If they don't get you in the wash, they'll get you in the rinse." McCrackin, a peace and civil rights activist for more than sixty years, now eighty-five years old, remains one of Mae Bertha's best friends.

On December 11, 1965, Mae Bertha wrote Jean Fairfax again:

> My husband went out today to get the settlement. We owe them $97 and were told to get off the place next week. Mr. Pemble's son-in-law told Matthew that if it had been left up to him we would have been put off in September. We don't have any place to go. Then Mr. Pemble spoke and said we could stay until we found a place, but he was going to sell the house. When you or someone come I will tell you everything. We need help.

The school bus driver and a teacher asked the children when they were moving, which confirmed Mae Bertha's suspicions of collusion between school officials and plantation owners. With cold weather setting in and eviction looming, Barbara Moffett, the director of the Community Relations Division of the AFSC, wired the U.S. commissioner of education:

> URGENTLY REQUEST YOUR OFFICE TAKE ACTION TO ENSURE THAT THE SEVEN CHILDREN OF MR. AND MRS. MATTHEW CARTER, R #1, BOX 37, MERIGOLD, MISS. CAN REMAIN IN DREW DISTRICT SCHOOLS. SINCE THE CARTERS ENROLLED THEIR SEVEN CHILDREN IN THE SCHOOLS THEY HAVE FACED CONTINUAL HARASSMENT INCLUDING HAVING THEIR HOME SHOT INTO. THEIR CHILDREN ARE THE ONLY NEGROES IN THIS PREVIOUSLY ALL-WHITE SCHOOL SYSTEM. THE

FAMILY NOW FACES EVICTION AND NEEDS THE SUPPORT AND HELP OF THE FEDERAL GOVERNMENT IN EXERCISING THEIR RIGHTS UNDER THE CIVIL RIGHTS ACT.

Jean Fairfax was named director of community programs for the NAACP Legal Defense and Educational Fund in New York City in late 1965, but continued a joint program for school desegregation with the AFSC in communities across the South. She worried a lot about the Carters and took it upon herself to contact the U.S. Department of Justice and the Farmers Home Administration for help in finding farmland or a house for the Carters. Mae Bertha traveled to Jackson where she met with attorney Marian Wright to devise a plan to keep the family in the school district. At Wright's suggestion, Mae Bertha applied to the local welfare department and the Farmers Home Administration, but was told at both agencies that there was no help available.

In mid-December, first-grader Deborah Carter wrote Jean Fairfax: "WE HAVE EATEN IN CAFETERIA. WE WISH YOU A MERRY CHRISTMAS."

Right before Christmas, the AFSC's Barbara Moffett wrote the Carters from Philadelphia and enclosed four postal money orders for one hundred dollars each, saying that they were a gift from the AFSC for rent or a down payment on a new home. Moffett wrote: "Your many friends here are thinking of you and your fine family at this holiday season. You are part of an important struggle to make the spirit of Christmas become real in all places at all times. We admire your courage. We send our Christmas love to you all."

WHEN WINIFRED Green and I first visited the Carters at Jean Fairfax's request in mid-January 1965, we also saw other black families who were experiencing similar harassment for choosing white schools. After returning to Atlanta, I acted in the Quaker tradition of "speaking truth to power" and sent the following telegram to President Lyndon Baines Johnson:

THIS IS TO INFORM YOU OF THE URGENT NEED FOR IMMEDIATE ACTION BY THE FEDERAL GOVERNMENT CONCERNING THE FAMILIES OF NEGRO CHILDREN NOW ATTENDING THE FORMERLY ALL WHITE SCHOOLS. ALL THESE FAMILIES BELIEVED THAT EQUAL OPPORTUNITIES (EDUCATIONAL) WOULD FINALLY BECOME A REALITY FOR THEIR CHILDREN UNDER TITLE VI OF THE 1964 CIVIL RIGHTS BILL AND THUS ENROLLED THEIR CHILDREN IN THE FORMERLY ALL-WHITE SCHOOLS IN SEPTEMBER. ON A VISIT TO MISSISSIPPI ON JANUARY 14–17, AS SOUTHERN FIELD REPRESENTATIVE OF THE AMERICAN FRIENDS SERVICE COMMITTEE, I TALKED WITH THESE FAMILIES. THESE FAMILIES HAVE FALLEN VICTIMS TO A CONSPIRACY DESIGNED TO DRIVE THEM FROM THEIR HOMES, DEPRIVE THEM OF THEIR LIVELIHOODS AND FORCE THEIR CHILDREN FROM THE PUBLIC SCHOOLS. HERE IS WHAT "FREEDOM OF CHOICE" MEANS . . .

I then described what had happened to the Carters and closed with:

SPEAKING FOR THE AFSC, I REQUEST THAT YOU, AS CHIEF EXECUTIVE, SEND IMMEDIATELY A TEAM OF INVESTIGATORS WHO ARE PREPARED TO EVALUATE THE SITUATION AND OFFER ASSISTANCE ON THE SPOT.

At the AFSC, we were never sure whether it was my telegram or someone else's that precipitated federal action, but in late January

1966, a Justice Department official came to Sunflower County and spoke with Mr. Pemble. Soon after, Matthew Carter was told that he could stay on another year sharecropping. He would have less land, however, and would only retain one-fourth rather than one-half of the cotton sales money.

During the early months of 1966, the national American Friends Service Committee office sent the Carters weekly checks from its Rights of Conscience Fund, which had been set up during the 1950s, in part to provide "sufferings grants" to individuals caught in the sweep of McCarthyism. By the early sixties, the fund was focused on the South, particularly after James Reeb, an AFSC staff member, was killed during the Freedom March in Selma, Alabama. A separate fund was also established, the James Reeb Memorial Fund, and then, in 1966, the Ford Foundation gave the AFSC a grant of $100,000 specifically for assistance to the many southern blacks who faced problems when they registered to vote or tried to enroll their children in white schools. At that point, the James Reeb Memorial Fund was renamed the Family Aid Fund and responsibility for its administration was shifted to me as southern field representative in Atlanta.

Before I was specifically assigned to Mae Bertha's case, she wrote every Monday to Eleanor Eaton or Marie Turner in Philadelphia.

Merigold, Mississippi
Route 1, Box 37
January 17, 1966

Dear Mrs. Eaton,

We received your letter and the money. We were glad to get the letter also the money. We are very happy you all are helping us

because they are out to get us here. It is so sad but true. Sometimes
I wonder how long are they going to last being mean. We don't
have a living here. But we don't have to move right now. That
means a lot. Yes we were glad to see Miss Curry she is real nice. I
wish I could see all of you. Our car out of the shop and I am glad
because we live too far to walk to town and I have to go there if
my kids get sick. I am listening to [Senator] Stennis from Mississippi. He so worry about Vietnam but have not said anything
about how people are treated here. He not worry about the
hungry here. We live here every day under fear. I hope he not talking about sending our boys to Vietnam until we get free here. I
feel so sorry for them. Anything Mississippi go out for it not good
for Negroes. Let me close. I could write a book about them.

Yours,
Mae Bertha Carter

Feb. 2, 1966

Dear Mrs. Eaton,

My husband said he was thinking he wouldn't take it up the
offer from Pemble for less land but this was the best we could do
at this time, so our kids could still stay in the school. So we won a
little and we don't have to move until fall at least. Maybe this will
give courage to other Negroes. They were so sure we had to move.
And we were going to be hungry. If we be able to stay in this
school, I believe many more children will go this fall. Some say
they may go. This free choice is not good. The people are so afraid.
But we going try to do some looking around for more land. We

didn't get any free food because our paper wasn't fixed up in time. Your boss man got to fix them up. I think you can tell about your income yourself, but no, the boss have to say it. Our car got to be checked before the 31 of March to see if it is good enough to be on the highway. That a Mississippi law and another way to get at the poor, because the rich all have good cars. Our car ten years old, I hope they will let it pass. I get so sad sometime but that's all in it. Just some people have given their life for freedom. I have been working first in the NAACP. Then I start going to SNCC meetings, then the FDP [Freedom Democratic party]. We sang we wasn't going to let these things turn us around. . . . I went to Church Sunday and I am still happy. Our Pastor really preached about how He came to his own and his own knew him not and when it was time for Him to be born there wasn't any room at the inn. I will close. I know you don't have time to read all this.

Yours Truly,
Mae Bertha Carter

When Marie Turner sent clothing for the children from the AFSC warehouse, Mae Bertha often responded with long and musing letters.

Feb. 7, 1966

Dear Mrs. Turner,

Your letter have been received and we are glad to hear from you at all times. It make us feel much better. So much worry. We came out with $40 from crops and we are going to give Mr. Bob at the store some of it. In times past we got more money a month than any family here. But now the least of the families here get as much as we do. It still cold here. They have not started to farm.

We used to plant cotton in the first of April but we don't do that any more. It is still too cold and too muddy nowadays. The kids doing so good in school and my first grader know so much more than my other first graders before, until I don't want them to ever go to another segregated school. We want to stay to give courage to the others here because the people around Drew living so far back in the past. I want to start a garden soon, if the man let us have some land. You can get so afraid here thinking about if you stop helping us what would happen. Once I had to eat meal mush and stay in bed to keep warm. This was when I was a child in the 30's and we wore dresses made out of the sacks we pick cotton in. I guess I close. Love to all of you.

Mae Bertha Carter

P.S. Yes Miss Falls will bring you down some time. I told her I would like to see you, if you like to come over. The package just came and I am happy to get the things. I will finish the dress you sent me. When you have as many girls I have, it nothing left for me, but I can change that now and I am happy. Thanks a lot.

In April 1966, Mae Bertha rode a chartered bus to Washington, D.C., with a group of southern blacks to demonstrate for housing, food, and jobs. I asked Mae Bertha for her sharpest memory of the demonstration: "It was that black schoolteacher that put us up at her house and took all the good food that the churches had provided— supposed to feed us—and then gave us hot dogs and crackers. And you know I wrote that woman and told her thank you for the bed and no thank you for keeping all that food and feeding us junk."

After the demonstration, Mae Bertha rode a Greyhound bus to

Philadelphia and spoke at the weekly AFSC staff meeting. She thanked everyone for their support. She remembers being very nervous, but told me that she always calmed down the minute she started describing the never-ending problems of keeping the children in school. Even though this trip was Mae Bertha's first visit to the Northeast, and her first speech to an assembled group, the highlight for her was the chance to meet Marie Turner and her husband, Paul, and to stay at their home. Many years later, I found in Marie Turner's files an envelope with Mae Bertha's return address. Inside the envelope was a scrap of paper with a message in Mae Bertha's handwriting, evidently written right after the trip, saying only, "I would like to be a Quaker."

Later in the month, Mae Bertha went to a joint AFSC-NAACP school desegregation meeting in Jackson intended to inform black parents of the 1966–67 federal school desegregation guidelines. Mae Bertha wrote that all of her children went with her to Jackson and were glad to meet people such as Lloyd Henderson of HEW who had done so much to help them. At the meeting, Mae Bertha testified about the hard times in Drew. Freedom of choice was not working, she said. She doubted that any other black children would go to white schools in Sunflower County in 1966. A new study of school desegregation in Mississippi that was released at the meeting showed that out of a total black student population of 274,900, only 928 (less than half of 1 percent) were in desegregated schools. The study, sponsored by the Mississippi Council on Human Relations, also reported that "over half of the Negro families with children in desegregated schools have been subjected to extensive harassment."

MAE BERTHA wrote her first letter to me in Atlanta in late April 1966, after her "transfer" from Philadelphia. For the next three years, until April 1969, the AFSC sent the Carters a twenty-five-dollar grant each Friday, and Mae Bertha responded each Monday to me or my assistant, Addie Ringfield.

In mid-May 1966, Mae Bertha was again invited north, to New York this time. Anna Frank, a longtime supporter of the NAACP Legal Defense and Educational Fund, wanted her to speak at a convocation on The Tragic Gap, at which she would be one of the panelists interviewed by the actor Ossie Davis. The headlines in the June 4 edition of *The Afro-American* described Mae Bertha's speech: "Mississippi Mother Cries—'If My Son Can't Go To School, Why Must He Go To Viet Nam.'" Mae Bertha told the group that "many boys in Mississippi join the Army, Air Force and Navy because they lack money and can't go to college and can't get a job in Mississippi."

Mae Bertha's second letter to me was about the problems on Busyline and her trip to New York. Her letters continued over the summer months and painted a vivid picture indeed.

May, 1966

Dear Mrs. Curry,

Your letter has been received and we were glad to get both the money and the letter. Yes it been raining here and the land been wet. My husband made only $16 last week plowing. The cotton about all planted now. The boss told my husband he was moving our acre of garden but have not told us where it was going to be and the small pasture where we had our cow is all plowed up. We will be needing the garden very much. I am very tired. Yes I enjoy myself in New York. The people were so good. Jean Fairfax was so sweet. Seem like I was in another world. The first day I ate dinner with one of the nicest white women in the world. The last day I was there another of the nicest white women in the world took me to United Nations. I hate to use the word white lady. I wish I could just say lady, but I just want you to know what I am talking about. Oh people were so nice. And little ole me riding on my first airplane. Yes I am still happy. I went to church on Sunday and my preacher preach about love one another—it don't mean Negro only—it means everybody, white and black. It feel so good to love. You don't feel good with hate. I am glad I love people, the Bible says love your enemies. You know Mrs. Granberry, my friend in Cleveland. We went to her girl's commencement service on Sunday May 20 with Ruth and Gloria and the Granberry kids and we were the only negroes there. So sad. We are going back on 23rd to the graduation. The people were nice and the preacher was good. I think it was an FBI man there because a man come up and talk with us, but he didn't say he was one.

Love,
Mae Bertha Carter

June 1, 1966

Dear Mrs. Curry,

We were glad to hear from you. Thanks a lot. With the kids out of school don't seem like I can fill them up. They were eating lunch at school I guess that's why. Yes the children all made

another grade and they are glad and so am I. They are chopping
cotton now. It not much for our family to chop. You see this
farmer put down this grass killer on his beans and cotton. This
means just a little chopping if any. We don't have the cow pas-
ture yet, so my husband said he was going on and tie her to the
side of the road. If my husband works this week, he will make 20
dollars and pay Mr. Bob ten dollars a month for food we got
before we enroll our kids in the schools. We went back to the
graduation on Tuesday night. This was the first time a Negro
had been to this place—the Walter Sillers Coliseum. Everybody
acted ok. They set all down beside us. You see, we were all
dressed up. Smile.

Love,
Mae Bertha Carter

June 14, 1966

Dear Miss Curry,

I feel some better. My husband and I went out today to vote for
the first time. You know I got afraid once because of the shooting,
but it passed away. Where we had to go vote at Mr. Bob's store, we
still owe money. My husband have a statement in his pocket.
Eaton [an AFSC staff member] met my husband. He like her. Oh
yes, the freedom of choice paper have come from the school and
we have fill them out and mail them in. We mark in the wrong
place again—the formerly white school. *Smile.* I hope this time it
won't be any shooting. I am thinking we are the only ones again. I
hope I am wrong. Work is up for my husband after today. I going
to pray today. The old saying—go as far as you can go and when

you get there maybe you can go farther. That's our motto. You be sweet. Love to Miss Falls.

Love,
Mae Bertha Carter

It was a terrible summer. In August, Eleanor Eaton, in an update for Barbara Moffett, reported that Mae Bertha had called and in the course of their conversation said that Drew police had gone to the Pemble place and killed a black man. There was no report in the newspaper and everyone seemed afraid to talk about it, so much so that Mae Bertha was even uncomfortable mentioning it over the phone. In July, Lloyd Henderson from HEW, along with Mae Bertha and three of his staff, had gone house to house in the black community in Drew to recruit children to enroll in the white schools—to no avail.

Mr. Pemble sent people to tear down the Carters' barn where their cow and hog were sheltered, even though Matthew had been unable to find land or a house to rent or buy. Mae Bertha's August letter to me reflected their further discouragement over money:

> We don't have a fall garden yet. The eight acres Mr. Pemble let us have, after we get through picking at the end of the year, will probably make about 8 bales of cotton. It should bring about a hundred and fifty dollars a bale. Half of the money goes to Mr. Pemble. We will have to pay all debts out of our half, such as the light bill, gas bill, poisons and plowing of the cotton. And we have to pay the $195 he let us have to live until we start to pick the cotton, then he will let us have $8 a bale to live on when we are picking. So what we have left? Nothing and school is coming. What we going to do?

The Carter's new house on Broadway, Drew, Mississippi.

Nine

I Felt So Proud

R esidents of Drew in general, and neighbors on one street in particular, woke to a surprise on October 1, 1966. During the early hours, the Carters had moved into a one-story frame house with green asbestos shingles on Broadway. The journey to their new address had taken more than a year and required the combined efforts of the AFSC, the NAACP Legal Defense and Educational Fund, and the Unitarian Universalist Association. The Carters, along with Marian Wright and other Defense Fund staff in Jackson, had begun looking for a new home for the family almost as soon as the children desegregated the Drew schools. Various attempts to purchase or rent a house in Drew had been met with closed doors at the very mention of the family's name.

In July 1966, Mel Leventhal, a young attorney from the Defense Fund office in Jackson, visited the Carters and learned that another potential home had just been sold the week before. Matthew told Mel of his fruitless attempts to find either a house or land to build on. Mel reported to Marian Wright, "I think it is quite clear that the Carters will not be able to purchase a house in their own name." In early August, Jean Fairfax asked a member of her staff, Allen Black, to go to Sunflower County and find a house for the Carters. Black, who had been active in school desegregation in his hometown of Florence, Alabama, was young, tall, charming, and African-American. Under the guise of a worker for the Unitarian Church, he was immediately shown eight or nine possible houses. In secret consultation with the Carters, the Broadway house was chosen, and Black began negotiations to buy it for seven thousand dollars from Mr. Willie Jones, who lived in Chattanooga, Tennessee. Black used his name for the purchase, and legal papers were drawn up later showing that the house was held "in trust" for the Carters.

"The house has a carport and attached utility room and is located on the edge of the Negro subdivision," Black wrote Eleanor Eaton. "There is an additional lot adjoining which can be used for a small garden. Inside, the house is in good repair. The walls in the living room, hall and all three bedrooms are of nicely varnished pine (just made for kids). There is a complete bathroom, central gas heat (floor furnace), additional gas outlets in each room, a quick recovery water heater and a vent over the kitchen range. The floors had once been painted but were of sufficient quality that a good wax job will make them quite presentable. The house contains furniture and Mr. Jones has offered to sell it for $200.00."

Back in Philadelphia, AFSC staff moved quickly to find funds to purchase the house. Barbara Moffett and Eleanor Eaton requested money from the AFSC Little River Farms Fund. The fund, totaling nine thousand dollars, was in a Philadelphia savings account and had been used for many years to help Wilmer and Mildred Young establish a cooperative farm in Abbeville, South Carolina. The Youngs had once worked at the Delta Cooperative Farm in Bolivar County, not far from the Carters' house on the Pemble Plantation, where they helped to relocate Arkansas sharecroppers who were threatened by violence and eviction for joining the Southern Farmer's Tenant Union in 1936. Now the Little River Farms Fund made a loan of thirty-five hundred dollars to help the Carters.

Eleanor Eaton suggested to the Unitarian Universalist Association that it contribute toward purchasing the house; and on August 29, the association advanced thirty-five hundred dollars to match the Little River contribution. Eaton sent a check for fifteen hundred dollars to Marian Wright for an immediate option on the house, and Wright and Allen Black worked through September to secure the purchase.

When Black arrived at Busyline on September 30, packing was well under way. The family was anxious over the secrecy about the move into Drew. They worried about new neighbors in Drew who might oppose their attempt to desegregate the schools. And Matthew worried about doing right by Mr. Pemble and gathering the last of the cotton crop he had raised. Bob Pope, the plantation storeowner, had agreed to take some of Matthew's peas as partial payment of his account. "We have to live with these people," Matthew told Black.

"Matthew was always wanting to be honest and do right," Mae Bertha later told me. "He started that crop and he wanted to finish it. Seems like he would take any kind of thing and he said to me, 'Mary, I have to be right.' That's all he said. And I said, 'Right?' *I* know right. The next thing, they'll be tearing the house down. I'm going to move and move now." That night everyone moved except Matthew. He stayed behind for a week until his cotton was picked.

After they got home from school on the designated moving day, Ruth, Gloria, and Larry rode into Drew with Allen Black to clean the new house, turn on the heat, and get the appliances working. Shortly after eight—just after dark—the rest of the family arrived, towing a canvas-covered trailer behind the old car. Since the house was already partially furnished, they had brought only a few large items; the rest was mostly personal belongings. That night Larry, the oldest son, went to bed torn between respect for his father's determination to honor the sharecropper's contract and fear for Matthew's safety out alone picking cotton on a deserted part of the plantation.

Larry later told me, "If it had been me, I would have left that cotton in the field." Then he laughed and said, "No, I probably would have done the same thing. Dad was committed to finish it up. He'd stay out there late at night and then be out early in the morning and he'd put his car way around back at night and turn off all the lights because he didn't want the white people to know he was out there by himself. And he wouldn't stay in Drew until he finished."

The house on Broadway was the nicest the Carter family had ever occupied, and Allen Black described them as being "in good spirits." He wrote Eleanor Eaton about the scare they had when Mayor Williford's insurance company canceled the policy on the house and the property was uninsured for twenty-four hours before Black could take out a policy with Allstate in Jackson.

The Carter daughters were particularly fond of Black, whom they described as "that tall, dark, handsome man," and most of the children called him Uncle Allen. When he went to the grocery store, he would make it a point to stock up on nutritional foods, saying that he was on a diet and required these special foods while he was staying with the Carters. "I'm always impressed," he wrote, "with the fierce pride they seem to have. Did you know that Matthew subsisted on tomatoes and milk the entire week he spent picking the last of the cotton. Things will be some better because Mr. Carter was able to slaughter a hog last week."

In December, the Carters signed a contract with the AFSC to repay thirty-five hundred dollars with no interest, beginning August 1, 1967, at the rate of thirty dollars per month. The Carters never missed a payment, and eight years later, in July 1975, the deed and title to the house on Broadway were transferred to their names. Mae Bertha still lives there.

When Eleanor Eaton visited the Carters in their new home for the first time, Mae Bertha was radiant: "I can't tell it in words how happy I was to get here. I was so glad to leave the farm, the plantation, and I don't know what it seemed like when I moved in this house—heaven, I think. When I got in the house I felt so proud. There was furniture in the house and then we owned a refrigerator and there was food in the refrigerator that Allen bought. And then I went on down the hall and opened a little door and that was the bathroom, and I had never been used to no bathroom. We had been going to the outside toilet. And then I looked and, oh my, the bathtub. All you had to do was run your water, your hot water and your cold water. You know we didn't have hot water and cold water before. Yes, seemed like heaven when I got here."

Stanley remembered the move to Drew as one of the best days of his life. Gloria and her sisters recalled their joy at never having to use an outhouse again. And most of all it meant an end to picking cotton, an end to tender, sore fingers cut by the sharp brown pods of the cotton boll. Twenty-eight year later, on a visit to Broadway, I showed Mae Bertha's six-year-old granddaughter Shayla a handful of cotton that I had picked up on the side of the road. Shayla looked at the boll, looked up at me, and said, "Did your fingers bleed when you picked it?" Mae Bertha was there, and she knew that Shayla would be the last Carter to carry that image.

Two weeks after moving into the new house, Mae Bertha wrote me, "I am sure the water bill will be up because the children love the bath and they want to bath two times a day. I can't keep any soap. We not used to plenty water, so you see this is a step to freedom, this is what freedom mean to me. Then some way to make money where we can eat three meals a day and my kids can go to school and keep a nice place to live. We have the house and pray we will have the rest soon."

One of Mae Bertha's prayers was answered in November when she found a job taking care of children in the Head Start program in nearby Cleveland. "It was right after we moved in here and I prayed and prayed," she told me. "I said, 'Now You know I need a job. My husband don't have a job and I don't have a job. So we can't depend on other people.' I got on the back porch for a while and I said that prayer and then something said, 'Get up, get up and go to Cleveland and see Mr. Amzie Moore.' Mr. Moore was on the board or something at Head

Start. He said, 'Oh I thought you would come. I've been looking for you.' And he got up and called the Head Start director and told him that I needed a job and he wanted him to place me somewhere. Then Mr. Moore told me, 'Okay, come back Monday and start to work.' I went back on Monday and I worked there for twenty-one years.

"Well, when we first started to work it wasn't no teacher's aides and teachers and like that. In years past, it changed into teachers and teacher's aides. I worked directly with the children. It was three of us to a unit at that time and about thirty children."

I asked Mae Bertha if she still liked working with children after having thirteen of her own—actually fourteen, counting Jean, the granddaughter who lived with her for eleven years. She replied, "Yes, I did. I really liked working with children the best of anything. The hardest part was I couldn't stay at home during the week, 'cause I didn't have transportation to Cleveland from Drew every morning. So after I got the job I started staying in Cleveland with my friend Willie Mae Johnson from Monday to Friday evening, then I come back home. I walked from Willie Mae's house every day, about a half mile, to Peter Rock Church. And then later on Naomi married L.C. and she was living in Cleveland and I started staying with them. I did that until my husband got a job working at the Head Start at Ruleville. By then we had an automobile and Matthew would bring me to Cleveland and then go on to his job, and then pick me up in the afternoon, so I got to go home every day.

"Now when I was staying in Cleveland for five days and Matthew had no job, he would cook for the children and then get their clothes ready for school and shine their shoes and all that. I told him, 'Don't worry, Matthew, don't worry about you don't have a job. You got a job, you just going to be the housewife, the house maid, or something. It was over a year before he got the Head Start job."

Although Matthew and Mae Bertha finally had full-time work with Head Start, many years passed before their jobs meant regular paychecks. Federal anti-poverty programs such as Head Start meant only one thing to the white establishment in the South in the 1960s—empowerment of black people. From its beginning in 1965, the Child Development Group of Mississippi, the first statewide Head Start program, was considered by most whites as evil incarnate. The editorial page of the *Jackson Daily News*, on May 1, 1965, carried an article entitled "A Look at 'Head Start'":

> There is a disquieting aura, almost terrifying in its ultimate projection, hovering wraith-like above the Head Start phase of the federal government's poverty program.
>
> Head Start is specifically designed to include children of all races and both sexes from one to six years of age, considered underprivileged and in need of guidance and direction in preschool preparation.
>
> On the face of this undertaking, it appears to be most wholesome and humane, appealing to the most tender senses in assisting infant youngsters who otherwise might be relegated to slum dwelling influence, undesirable home background and lack of basic necessities.
>
> However, as all federal programs are now designed, here is one of the most subtle mediums for instilling the acceptance of racial integration and ultimate mongrelization ever perpetrated in this country.

The editorial went on to describe the "most frightening parallels"—Soviet Russia, Red China, and Hitler's Germany—all of which "separate children from their parents and indoctrinate them to the rigid doctrines of political leaders." White southern politicians employed every conceivable method either to eliminate Head Start programs or to put barriers in their way. In Washington, Senator John Stennis from Mississippi delayed Head Start appropriations. He charged that the Mississippi program misused funds and claimed that it was a front for hiring civil rights workers rather than child development professionals. Local appropriations were also held up, either in the state legislature or on the governor's desk. At the local level, Head Start employees were laid off for weeks or asked to work without pay. In both Bolivar and Sunflower counties, there was constant agitation by whites against the program. After a few years, the programs where Matthew and Mae Bertha worked stopped operating in the summer from lack of funds. Through all of this, Matthew and Mae Bertha struggled to feed, clothe, and shelter their family, which in 1966 grew to include their nine-month-old granddaughter Sylvia Jean, called Jean, after Jean Fairfax.

Letter to author from Mae Bertha Carter, 1967.

Ten

Really in the Dumps Now

Although 1966 brought the Carters the security of a house in Drew and Mae Bertha's job with Head Start, the family was beset by continuing problems at school and constant worry about money. Mae Bertha's 1967 New Year's Day letter to my office showed both her hope and discouragement:

> The New Year is here and the old one has passed. We can't help but think about all of you that help us get over the year and we write to say thanks. We can't say in word how much it means to us and we shall never forget you all. You are so good to us and are

here in Drew in this fight with us. We are hoping 67 will be much
happier for all of us and it will mean peace on earth, good will to
all men and our boys come home from Viet Nam, and I be able to
work and my husband get a job or something. We supposed to go
to work on the 3rd of January, if I am one of the lucky ones and I
hope so. I want to go to school very bad. They have an OEO
[Office of Economic Opportunity] Employment office here. My
husband went there. They told him he was too old. But men older
than him work and get welfare check. I don't know why they still
let Sunflower County get all that money. You have to be a good
nigger to get any of it. You got to be on welfare or a real good
nigger. Oh yes, they have a Headstart here in Drew. When they
were getting it up they sent people special invitations to come to
the meeting. I didn't get one. The superintendent of the schools
told them what he was going to do for them. But if they don't like
you, they will punish you—if you get out of line with their way of
life. They don't know about this up in Washington.

In March, Mae Bertha wrote me about the public library:

I am very sad. The teacher at the school told the children to go to
the public library to get a book. My kids—*poor kids* were thinking
this went for them too. So they went to the library. The lady gave
them cards, but she had news for them—they had to be signed by
a reference. They had to be here in Drew—men like Sunflower
food store management. We went in to see if this were true. It was.
Plus the board had to approve them. My girls ask if they could
come in to study. Well, she said the place too small. I am sure we
are first Negroes to go to this library, but it got to be done by

someone. Matthew have not heard from job yet. This still stands—
you got to be a good nigger here. We just can't be good niggers.
(Smile).

The greatest excitement in the family that spring was Ruth Carter's
anticipated graduation from Drew High School on May 23. Mae
Bertha invited all her friends from Atlanta and Philadelphia. At the
AFSC we had begun to work on scholarships and college plans for
Ruth when we heard from Mae Bertha:

> I am writing you. I am very sad. I don't know what to do. Ruth is
> crying because at the last minute Friday her teacher told her she
> had failed English four points and wouldn't be able to graduate.
> She is so sad because she feels like they shouldn't have had her go
> through so much—the marching and also letting her bring her
> gown home. I hope you or some of your staff write Ruth—maybe
> she would feel better.

Ruth's depression over her failure to graduate weighed upon all of
us at AFSC, and in the middle of June the national office arranged for
her to attend a high school work camp at the Coal Branch Heights Project in West Virginia. After the work camp, Ruth went to Toledo, with
no plans to go back to Drew to complete the required hours for graduation. In September, however, Ruth changed her mind and returned to
finish at Drew High School.

In June 1967, Larry Carter wrote to Sargent Shriver, the director of
the Office of Economic Opportunity in Washington, D.C., and asked
for help getting into Upward Bound, a federally funded academic
enrichment program. Theodore Berry from Shriver's office told Larry

that they would get him in the program and encouraged him to perse-vere: "Perhaps, if you continue to do as well as you have done in the past, you can help solve some of the problems of our country." Larry was enrolled in Upward Bound at Tougaloo College for six weeks and traveled to New Mexico as part of the program.

Almost daily the Carters questioned whether they would have enough money to live on. Matthew looked for work and met one rejec-tion after another. He stayed busy taking care of the children and for several months he and Naomi registered voters in Sunflower County in a drive sponsored by Fannie Lou Hamer. Hamer had requested that federal voter registrars be sent to Sunflower. She cited the large major-ity of eligible black voters who were not registered, and the county's history of resistance to civil rights activities, as reasons for the federal presence. The registrars never came. Washington told local black leaders that there was too much pressure from Senator James East-land, who would be embarrassed by this kind of face-off in his home county. Nevertheless, Hamer traveled throughout the county to raise money to register voters; she paid registration workers like Matthew twenty-five dollars a week plus mileage. Matthew told Mae Bertha how discouraging and difficult it was to sign up black people on the plantations: "I would go there at night and they would promise to be ready to go register the next morning and there wouldn't be a soul around when I went to pick them up, or they'd be sick in bed."

In July 1967, Matthew was finally hired for a federally funded "work experience" program in Drew. When Matthew reported to work on the first day, he was immediately sent home. Chief of Police Curtis Floyd informed him that he could not work for the program because he had a suit pending against the city. Mae Bertha and

Matthew assumed he was talking about their suit against the Drew school district, filed the month before to bring about further school desegregation. Allen Black wrote a letter of complaint to the U.S. Department of Health, Education and Welfare:

> Mr. Carter, like most of us who believe what we read, operated under the assumption that participation in the work experience program was not contingent upon the acquiescent and sub-servient acceptance of the status quo but upon the fact that one is needy. Mr. Carter, a mild and gentle man, believed that federal programs designed to enhance the employability of poverty stricken adults would operate on such a basis to insure his rights as a citizen and to better his economic status.

By the time the complaint was investigated, Matthew had found another job.

When the Carters applied for food stamps, Mae Bertha met excuses about eligibility and was discouraged by the application procedures and questions. Matthew in turn was asked about the weekly letters he received from the AFSC, and when he told about the twenty-five-dollar weekly grants, the agency personnel asked for a statement from the AFSC on the amount and uses of the grant. I hastily wrote and reminded the Sunflower County food stamp program that gifts from church and service organizations are not figured into the determination of a family's eligibility. Mae Bertha wrote me in August:

> These people don't want us to have food stamps. They don't want anybody to give us any money. They are planning on running us out of Mississippi. This is what my husband thinks. A man came

to see him about this job. A friend told my husband—the friend
works on this job—that there was a meeting about Matthew and
the job. One man said they don't have to hire him because we get
so much money each month. The friend told my husband please
don't say anything about this. My husband feels like if they would
let him work, then no one would have to give him anything and
we wouldn't go hungry. They are saying we get paid to send our
kids to school. This is so sad, but when you are a Negro you have
to suffer all this. Some time my husband feel like he can't go on.
He has always worked so hard for his family—now the whites
around here trying to see who helps us and why Matthew don't
need to work. All for now, I don't feel well, I have a cold.

Mae Bertha wrote me in September:

Here is the money for the first two payment for August and September on the house. I been so busy with the kids going back to
school—so much to get ready I got a headache. Ruth is back. My
baby Carl going now. The tension is high in Drew. Matthew took
the kids to school as he always do. A white man came to car, ask
him who he was and had he talked to good Lord on what he was
doing. Do you think your children should go to the Negro school
and did he think his children was better than the other Negro kids
and then he said your kids can get just as good education at the
other school. I know that you are doing it for money. My husband
told him he did it because of the freedom of choice papers. The
man said the papers didn't mean anything. Matthew told the man
not to tell him what kind of education the children will get at the
Negro school because he had five to finish there. My husband said

he couldn't say too much with all the whites around. Then the man went in the school when he stop talking to Matthew.

When Eleanor Eaton visited the Carters in 1967, the report she sent back caused the AFSC to worry that the family might be nearing the end of its patience; Eaton wondered whether the Carters could continue to live in Drew. Early in 1968, when Mae Bertha received letters of concern from the AFSC and the Boulder Friends Meeting, she was quick to say that there must have been some misunderstanding: they did *not* want to move to another county. The family had finally been approved for food stamps, she had just been promoted to resource teacher, the children had all done well on their midterm exams, and Ruth and Larry were supposed to graduate in May—the first black students to graduate from Drew High School in the history of Sunflower County.

IN MARCH 1968, Dr. Martin Luther King, Jr., came to the Delta. The Carters went to hear him speak at the New Hope Baptist Church in Cleveland. Mae Bertha was thrilled. She said she always stopped whatever she was doing when Dr. King came on the radio or television, because it was like music when he spoke—he knew what needed to be done to help people. With members of the Southern Christian Leadership Conference (SCLC), King was recruiting for the Poor People's Campaign, which was his first attempt to combine the fight for racial justice with the larger issues of economic disparity. As part of the campaign, the organizers were planning a "mule train" that would begin in Marks, Mississippi, and gather people into the march along the way to Washington. The SCLC was working to include other groups in the demonstration in Washington, such as the farm workers in California led by Cesar Chavez, Native-American organizations, labor unions, and white groups working for economic justice.

Dr. King asked the AFSC to pledge its commitment to the march for the Poor People's Campaign. I was designated as AFSC liaison for the planning meetings in Atlanta. One of his requests to us was to help recruit marchers through our contacts in southern black communities. So, during the spring of 1968, Winifred Green and I spread the word about the campaign.

Once, in March, on my way to visit the Carters, I stopped in Grenada, Mississippi, to see Leon Hall, a friend of mine and an SCLC organizer from Atlanta who was recruiting in the Delta. That evening, King came through on a whirlwind tour and spoke at a mass meeting. Afterward, Hall decided to ride with me to Drew and then back to Jackson. For a black man to ride in the same car with a white woman was still foolhardy in Mississippi, and we left Grenada around dark, planning to stop and spend the night with Milburn Crowe in all-black Mound Bayou, not far from Drew. In Mound Bayou, Leon and I stopped at a storefront—the Crowe's Nest. It was a store and restaurant as well as a meeting and gathering place for local and visiting movement people. We went inside where I met Crowe, one of Mound Bayou's longtime activists, who fed us some unforgettable barbecue ribs and then took us through a curtain-covered door to the back of the store where a poker game was in progress. Leon Hall and I had played in some Atlanta games, so we poured ourselves a little scotch and joined in. I look back on that night when I sat with five black men and gambled and drank in the middle of Mississippi, and all I can say is, "It seemed perfectly fine at the time." It did, and it really was, because of the insulation and protection of the all-black town. Driving through Mound Bayou twenty-three years later, I was happy to find that the Crowe's Nest and Milburn Crowe were still there. My sister Ann was with me recently when I went in to see Mr. Crowe. We talked for a while and he did indeed remember me and the poker game. Ann could barely believe the story. I told her that I was just happy I hadn't been given Winifred Green's campaign-related assignment—checking to see if mules were fit to join the "train" to Washington by looking in their mouths to determine the condition of their teeth!

MARTIN LUTHER King, Jr., was still planning the Poor People's Campaign when he decided to go to Memphis to help with the sanitation workers' strike in April 1968. We held a campaign strategy meeting in the basement of Ebenezer Baptist Church in Atlanta the night before he left for Memphis. I remember shaking Dr. King's hand and telling him goodbye and to be careful in Memphis. The next day, April 4, he was assassinated on the balcony of the Lorraine Motel, where he and his staff were staying.

Mae Bertha was very depressed over King's death and wrote to us, "I am very sad, and I am so afraid, but someday we *will* overcome. The world has suffered a great loss. Martin Luther King—we loved him, but God loved him best." Although Mae Bertha wanted desperately to go on the march to Washington for the Poor People's Campaign, in the end she decided against it. She did not want to risk her job by taking the time off, nor did she want to miss Ruth's and Larry's May graduation from Drew High School.

On June 3, 1968, when Robert Kennedy was assassinated during his campaign for the presidency, Mae Bertha and I commiserated over the phone, and later she wrote me of her admiration for both Robert and John F. Kennedy:

> John Kennedy—I knew when he was campaigning to be the President that he was concerned about white people and black people and all races of people and during his speeches I heard that he was concerned about education for black children. So I always thought he was the best President for this country and the best one I had ever lived under. Now I liked Truman because on the economics, he wanted everybody to have a good living in the United States, but John Kennedy was my best. And now Bobby Kennedy's gone too.

Mae Bertha had read about Bobby Kennedy's visit to Mississippi in 1966 when he told five thousand people crowded into the University of Mississippi coliseum, "We must create a society in which Negroes will be as free as other Americans—free to vote, and to earn their way, and to share in the decisions of government which will shape their lives." She reminded me that he had come to the Delta in spring 1967 and that she had met him at the Cleveland Head Start center. She described him as being so "quiet and gentle and interested in everything we were doing."

The NAACP attorney Marian Wright had been responsible for bringing Kennedy and other senators to Mississippi in 1967. Later, when Kennedy was running for president, Wright recalled that visit: "He did things that I wouldn't do. He went into the dirtiest, filthiest, poorest black homes . . . and he would sit with a baby who had open sores and whose belly was bloated from malnutrition, and he'd sit and touch and hold those babies. . . . I wouldn't do that! I didn't do that! But he did. . . . That's why I'm for him."

I had met Robert Kennedy myself in Jackson when he returned from that trip to the Delta. I was as drawn to him as Mae Bertha and Marian Wright were. We all felt that Robert Kennedy understood the plight of poor people in the Delta, and he signified hope. After his death, Mae Bertha wrote me:

> I am really in the dumps now. I am so worried losing Mr. Kennedy. I don't know what we going to do now. I am so sad and can't believe it's true. Seems like we don't have choices now. I didn't feel like going to work, I stayed up so late to get the news. Seems like our best men gone and left us all alone. We loved Mr. Kennedy. He was a wonderful man—a man whose only concern was his fellow man but like Dr. King, the Lord loved him best. He took him home to rest. I know he was tired. You know you get tired sometime working for justice and don't seem like you getting anywhere. I feel like this is just the beginning of sorrow for us here in America. I hope I am wrong. After all of this—surely a brighter day on the way.

Twenty-two years later, in November 1990, Mae Bertha and I were reminded of Robert Kennedy when Maxwell Taylor Kennedy—his youngest son—walked into my living room in Charlottesville, Virginia. I was in Charlottesville as a postdoctoral fellow at the Carter G. Woodson Institute's Center for the Study of Civil Rights at the University of Virginia, and an old friend from SNCC, Julian Bond, was teaching a course on the history of the movement that fall. We had invited Mae Bertha and her friend Winson Hudson to visit the university, as guests of the institute, and to speak in Julian Bond's class. I had known Winson Hudson since 1964, when she helped lead the school desegregation battle in Mississippi's Leake County, where she lived.

Max Kennedy was a second-year law student at the University of Virginia that semester. He is tall, strong, and looks very much like his father. That fall morning when I told my two friends from Mississippi that Max Kennedy was at the university and wanted to meet them, they rushed around the house dressing, and for about ten minutes before his arrival they disappeared back in the bedroom.

After warm embraces and introductions, Max sat down on the couch. Mae Bertha was looking at him intently: "Your daddy could have spit you out whole." Max threw back his head and laughed. Both women told him of meeting Robert Kennedy and of how much hope he had brought to black people. And Mae Bertha told him about playing John Kennedy's speech out on the porch when the overseer tried to get her and Matthew to withdraw their children from the white school in 1965.

Winson told Max about being with Medgar Evers the night before he was murdered in 1963 and that "he knew he might be killed, just like your daddy knew he might be killed." The women said they had something they wanted to sing for Max, and they took out pieces of paper they had prepared in the back room and began to sing the 1960s song "Abraham, Martin and John":

> Has anyone here seen my old friend Abraham,
> Can you tell me where he's gone?
> He freed a lotta people, but it seems the good die young,
> I just looked around and he was gone.

There they sat—Mae Bertha Carter, the tiny, light-skinned, blue-eyed mother of thirteen, a cotton sharecropper, one hand clasped over her heart as she sang, and Winson Hudson, tall, dark, imposing, cane at her feet, sitting straight in her chair, both singing in strong, sure voices to Max Kennedy, the twenty-five-year-old son of Robert, one of their many fallen heroes. On they went through the next two verses: "Has anyone here seen my old friend Martin. . . . Has anyone here seen my old friend John. . . . Can you tell me where they've gone?" Then, looking at the paper in their hands, they sang:

> Has anyone here seen my old friend Bobby?
> Can you tell me where he's gone?
> I thought I saw him walkin' up over the hill,
> With Abraham, Martin and John.

Through my tears I looked over at Max, who was struggling with his emotions. Listening to the two strong voices singing, all of us in the room felt courage, dreams, disappointment, and tragedy meet on a realm that transcended age, race, and riches.

BY THE beginning of school in 1968, Matthew was working at the Ruleville Head Start program, Mae Bertha was getting paid for her Head Start work, and Larry had received a scholarship from the Herbert Lehman Fund in New York and was enrolled at the University of Mississippi. Ruth needed to fulfill a science requirement for course work that had never been offered her in high school, and the Boulder Friends Meeting had sent a gift of $150 to help her with expenses for commuting to Coahoma Junior College in Clarksdale, which offered the course. By this time, the Boulder Friends were committed to seeing the battle through with the Carters. Their initial 1965 contribution of $30 a month for lunch money had expanded to $55 by the fall of 1968. Ruth and Gloria had attended a high school world affairs conference in Boulder the previous summer and had stayed with some Quaker families there. A representative of the Boulder Friends, Mary Jo Uphoff, began to correspond directly with me about the continuing needs of the Carters.

One of Mae Bertha's concerns that fall was the election of Richard Nixon as president. "The children are sad, all my co-workers are sad," she wrote. "Seems like there's no hope."

In many ways, though, 1969 was a better year for the Carter family. In the spring, Mae Bertha started going to classes every Saturday in Cleveland to prepare for the GED test. She wrote that she was afraid of the test, but that attaining a high school equivalency degree was something she had dreamed about. In the middle of April, both Mae Bertha and Matthew passed the test. Matthew's and Mae Bertha's salary payments continued to fluctuate with the politics of Head Start funding to Mississippi, and the family continued to live on a shoestring. In April, I had to write Mae Bertha that the AFSC would be discontinuing the twenty-five-dollar weekly grant because of cutbacks in our own funding. Mae Bertha continued to send us monthly house payments and we looked forward to her letters, which always faithfully described what was happening to the family, to Drew, to Mississippi, and often to the country.

Tension was high in Drew during the summer of 1969 because the court was finally preparing to hand down its decision in the Carters' suit against the Drew school system, filed in 1967 by Marian Wright of the NAACP Legal Defense and Educational Fund. The decision required that *all* elementary schoolchildren were to attend the A. W. James Elementary School starting in September 1969. Before the final court hearing in June, Mae Bertha wrote that the police chief's wife was "taking papers out to Negroes saying they don't want to go to the white schools. They got a lot of Negroes to sign their names. They are telling them we are the cause of all the mess."

That summer Mae Bertha joined a group of thirty black parents and children and one white teacher from the South who demonstrated at the U.S. attorney general John Mitchell's office in Washington. The trip was organized by the AFSC and the bus stopped at various towns on the way to Washington to pick up parents who were part of the demonstration group. The *Washington Post* reported that the group, after "riding a thousand miles by bumpy bus," waited for six hours at the attorney general's office and refused to leave without seeing him. The photograph in the *Post* showed Mae Bertha, purse on one arm, head cocked, with her feet firmly planted in front of John Mitchell's empty desk. When the demonstrators finally met with Mitchell, they told him of the harassment since integration and their fears that the administration was not supporting its own desegregation policies.

When school started in the fall of 1969, Beverly reported to her mother that all the black children assigned to her grade at A. W. James were in the same class! Deborah and one other child were the only blacks placed in an otherwise all-white class. Only two black teachers were at the school, and they taught the all-black classes. Mae Bertha was dumbfounded and called Mel Leventhal at Marian Wright's office in Jackson. When Mae Bertha called the school superintendent, "he was so nasty and said he would do what he wanted to and change things when he got good and damn ready."

That same week, Stanley brought home a letter from the principal saying he would be sent home if he didn't shave off his mustache. Stanley went ahead and shaved, but Mel Leventhal added this school "regulation" to the list of grievances against the Drew school system.

AFTER READING one of Mae Bertha's particularly moving letters in 1970, I had written in the margin, "After the courage, it's just endurance." By the 1970s, Mae Bertha was concentrating on community organization and continuing the constant battle with the school system. "I am working very hard on community affairs," she wrote me. "We are trying to promote the welfare rights and we are not pleased about how they using Title I money here in Drew. But we will have a hearing on Title I and still working on it. The Head Start program in Sunflower closed down because our Governor John Bell Williams vetoed the grant."

In April, Mae Bertha wrote:

Well, State Head Start got its grant, but if it isn't one thing it's another. John Bell Williams got all upset and he has set up qualification for all Head Start workers and it seems like he's going to have his way. It's hard when you are poor, uneducated and black. If black people don't get to heaven when they die, there's no hope here. So this is where we stand. John Bell Williams don't care anything about black children. He wants to hurt poor black people, cut us down where we will bow to them again. Nixon don't care too much for black people either. White people elected him. And Nixon trying to fix it where college boys will have to go to war. He mad with them so he send them to the army. If Nixon gets president the next term, I don't know what's going to happen to the USA. Maybe we'll all be dead.

Eleanor Eaton and I visited the Carters in June and felt that their situation might at long last be stabilizing. That summer, Larry went to summer school at the University of Mississippi, Ruth attended an AFSC work camp in Jamaica, and Gloria went to a summer program at Soul City in North Carolina. Stanley had graduated from high school and, like Larry, had received a scholarship from the Herbert Lehman Fund in New York to attend the University of Mississippi. The fund was specifically interested in giving scholarships to black students attending newly desegregated universities.

By September 1970, the year that Drew High School was fully integrated, most of the white children in Drew left the public school system and moved to segregated private academies. Mae Bertha wrote us about her concerns: "We heard the white people here plan on using the National Guard place here for children to go to private school, and I was told they moved the air conditioners out of the schools—said the booster club paid for them. We heard they're taking the football and athletic equipment from the schools for white children at the private schools. I don't know. I feel like it going to be a lots going on here that we don't know."

Later in the fall, Mae Bertha wrote that Governor John Bell Williams had once again refused to sign the papers to fund Head Start programs in the state. She was worried that the grants would be returned to Washington where things were just as bad. Nixon "doesn't need to be president of anything," she wrote.

By the end of December, Matthew's Head Start program had been closed down with no date set for reopening. The progress made by Freedom Summer, by civil rights legislation, and by federal anti-poverty programs was seriously threatened by a local bureaucracy intent on perpetuating racial and economic segregation. Mae Bertha understood the dynamic well: "Seems like we are on our way back. White people here can do anything they want to. If your black and you say anything about it you be sorry. Right now I don't see nothing good for poor people, black or white. The school is a mess, books going with the white children, and I am afraid before this is over, some people going to suffer. Sometimes you feel like forgetting it all, flying away and never coming back. Then you don't have nowhere to fly to—so much fighting going on."

IN LATE May 1971, Joetha Collier, one of Gloria's classmates, was shot to death in front of a grocery store not far from the Carter's house. Joetha and Gloria had just graduated from Drew High School the night before, and Joetha had won a good citizenship award at the ceremony. Her white principal had described her as a black student but "a good girl." Mae Bertha felt that the suspects, three white men, were just out looking for a black person to kill and that they might never come to trial because of legal technicalities. The Southern Christian Leadership Conference sent staff to investigate, and Mae Bertha went to SCLC meetings. Protest marches and demonstrations were organized, thirty-seven people were arrested, and the threat of violence caused Mayor Williford to impose a curfew. Black leaders viewed Joetha's murder against the backdrop of rising hostility in the white community. A successful voter registration drive was taking place in the Delta and an increasing number of black children were going to the previously white schools.

Freedom Summer *was* bearing fruit. Now Delta blacks understood that they too were citizens; they were voting; their children were graduating from high school and going to college; and a killing that might have gone unnoticed in Drew in the past now sparked demonstrations.

Mae Bertha wrote that after Joetha's shooting the family had become afraid, and she was dismayed about the private school proposed for Drew and about the shootings at Jackson State, the black university in Jackson, where local policemen and National Guardsmen had confronted black students during a civil rights demonstration on campus. Two students were killed and twelve wounded.

Mae Bertha wrote:

We hear a private school is going up here at Drew. Lord help these people. I wonder when are people going to learn color don't have anything to do with it. People are people. There are some rich people and some poor people, some able to eat some not, some have soap and hot and cold water, some had a chance to go to school, some didn't. Most of this can be corrected. I can't understand why the USA care so much for people far away and don't care anything for people around them. Folk from far away can come here and we send money to help them go to our schools and colleges. The USA is so crazy about them until they send our boys over there to die for them. Black boys, white boys, I can't understand this. Black boys now in two wars, the one overseas and the one in Jackson, Miss. If we don't do what they want us to do or don't think like they want us to, they will kill us. All we want to be is a citizen of the U.S. All for now, I am so fullup. Just had to put it on paper I guess. May the Lord bless all of us.

At the end of the school year, Mae Bertha discovered that her grand-daughter Jean had been going to preschool rather than the first grade. When Mae Bertha talked to the principal about this, he told her that he had given Jean a test and that she wasn't ready for the first grade. Mae Bertha was furious and told him, "I am tired of white people planning for our kids and not letting the parents know about it." This was the beginning of a long fight over the grading system and testing patterns. She wrote us, "If Jean wasn't ready for first grade, why didn't he tell me. I found out he set up a whole black class and said they weren't ready for first grade. I knew he had some five-year olds going to another school under Title I. Then he slipped Jean in and I didn't know it. I would like to write someone about this but I don't know who."

An encouraging event that summer was a visit to the Carters by Hank and Karen Zentgraf and their three daughters. Karen had been the Carters' contact person for the Boulder Friends Meeting for several years. She wrote the national AFSC office after the visit:

It seems impossible to give a comprehensive report of our four-hour visit with the Carters. Even if all that we saw and heard could be reported, the warmth, love and hospitality which the Carters extended to us would be missing. And that was the most wonderful part of the visit. . . . We met the grand-daughter, Sylvia Jean, whom they call Jean after Jean Fairfax, who has been living with the Carters since she was nine-months old. She is now seven years old.

The situation in the schools has changed since integration. Before, there were four school buildings in the community—the black and white versions of K–8 and 9–12 grades. With integration one of the black buildings was condemned. The remaining three school buildings are now used for the integrated elementary, junior high and senior high schools. When the schools first were integrated, the racial balance was perhaps 50-50. This year there were very few whites in the public schools because Sunflower Academy, a private school is providing segregated education for the whites. Mae Bertha feels that some of the whites are going hungry in order to send their kids to the school and that eventually they will be starved back into the integrated public school system.

Mae Bertha and Matthew gave the Zentgrafs a tour of the Pemble Plantation, their old home on Busyline, Mound Bayou, and Ruleville, describing various events from their lives all along the way. Karen reported that the tour was the best social studies lesson she'd ever had and said, "I feel sorry for anyone who has not visited the Carters." Later that summer, Beverly and Pearl went to visit the Zentgrafs in Colorado.

"SHE DOESN'T Give Up Easily," read the headline of a story in the *Delta Democrat Times* on February 25, 1973. The story told of Mae Bertha's continuing fight with the Drew school board and the formation of a Drew NAACP chapter. Mae Bertha was elected vice chair of the branch.

The black community in Drew received another blow when the court denied a temporary injunction to prevent school officials from enforcing a dress code. About fifty Drew High School students, including Deborah and Beverly, were suspended for violating the code. The suit, filed by Mae Bertha, charged that the dress code discriminated against black students. During the court hearing, an eleventh-grade student, James Young, said he wore an Afro because no white man should tell a black man how to wear his hair. The judge had Young's hair measured and reported it to be two and a half inches on the side and three and a half inches at the top. Several girls testified that they had been sent to the principal's office and been forced to kneel on the floor on a white piece of paper to have their dresses measured. Mae Bertha told the judge that the dress code "was doing something to the children mentally. They say they don't feel good anymore when they have to be measured."

Mae Bertha wrote me:

A few of the children are going back to the school. They are afraid. They had to promise not to protest any more. The superintendent told them if they ever protest again he was going to put them out of the school for good. I don't think this is right. They have this constitutional right to protest. They can't wear no clothes that don't match. If they wear pants, it have to be a suit with the top down below the hip. Every day the dresses are measured in every class. Deborah was sent home three times while I was at work. I asked him don't send her home alone. It didn't do any good. Also Head Start staff is trying to push people like me out of the program. It came out in the paper what we were doing about our children and four people from center staff came in and jump on me in front of everybody on where is my lesson plan. This is not right—other people lesson plans not as good and some don't even have one.

That spring, black parents appealed to the Drew board of aldermen, asking that a black be appointed to the all-white, all-male, five-member school board. Despite the protest, William DuBard was reappointed by the aldermen for another five-year term. What most angered the black community was that none of the school board members had their children in the public schools. By then, 80 percent of the Drew High School students were black.

Deborah and Beverly Carter (at left) with two college
friends at "Ole Miss" dormitory, 1978.

Eleven

Well Here I Am, Hello Again

Over the years, seven of the eight Carter children who desegregated the Drew schools graduated from the University of Mississippi. "Ole Miss," a nickname the university acquired in 1896, conjures
up images of white aristocracy, southern belles, magnolias, mint
juleps. During the Civil War, the university closed when the entire student body—all-male in those days—withdrew to join the Confederate army. To this day the football team is called the Rebels. But the
school is most famous—or infamous—for a bloody riot in 1962
prompted by the admission of its first black student; white Mississippians fought hard to preserve the university's "purity." In September

1962, when James Howard Meredith, a black Mississippian, attempted to enroll at the all-white university, Governor Ross Barnett physically blocked his admission, and when federal marshals escorted Meredith onto campus, white mobs incited by the governor went on a rampage. During a night of violence, two people were killed. President Kennedy had to send in troops to protect Meredith and restore order.

In 1968, Larry became the first of the Carter children to enroll at Ole Miss. By then the threat of racial violence had eased and fifty-three black students had been admitted. Nonetheless, that seven of the Carter children chose to attend this bastion of segregation is part of the family's remarkable story.

Larry graduated in 1972, and Carl, the last Carter child to enroll, graduated in 1982. All seven of the children who attended Ole Miss told me that their overall experiences there were positive and that they are glad they went.

AT HIS high school graduation rehearsal, Larry overheard several of his white classmates talking. He recalled, "They said, for my benefit, that at least they wouldn't have to go to school with me anymore. So when I got to Ole Miss and saw two of them, I said, 'How are you doing?' They said, 'There he is again.' But it was different. The hardest part was being away from home and living in the dormitory, but I got used to that, and I had a black roommate, which I guess was necessary because white kids left immediately if there was a black in their room. There were about fifteen blacks in my class. We organized a black student union and we'd get together in a little place in the student union building, and we had a place off campus where we gathered. I went to a few football games and some basketball games. We didn't have any black players on the Ole Miss teams then, and we'd go and root for the team that had black players. Did that upset the white students! But we were basically protesting.

"I majored in accounting mostly because I had done well in book-keeping and in Mrs. Stancill's math classes in high school. Of course classes were harder at Ole Miss and I had to study a lot more. Overall my experience was good. There was discrimination there, of course, but it was not overt.

"Now I did go to jail one night in 1970, my sophomore year. We were protesting the lack of black faculty members, black literature courses, and black football and basketball players and members of the student council. *Surely they could find a black football player.* So *we* had a rally one night and then we marched into a concert without paying. When we came out the city police were there to take us downtown. We spent the night in jail and some local people bailed us out. It never came to trial, so the charges must have been dropped. After I graduated in 1972, I wanted to leave Mississippi. I went to Boulder, Colorado, and stayed with Karen Zentgraf for awhile, but I couldn't find a permanent job, so four months later I joined the air force."

Stanley followed Larry to Ole Miss, majored in business, and graduated in 1974. Gloria enrolled in 1970 after graduating with honors from Drew High School. She made the dean's list three of her four years at Ole Miss. "I basically went to Ole Miss because I had two brothers who went before me. It was different in that you didn't get spitballs thrown at you and get called 'nigger' every day, but there was still no communication and many times I would still be the only black in the class. And I would sit there as a loner and in that respect it wasn't different. I had a black roommate and that made it better because at least outside of class you had people to talk to. And I loved having friends at school for the first time and we'd talk and laugh. The few blacks there stuck together and we had lots of fun. Also, I felt the quality of education would continue to be pretty good—Ole Miss had a good reputation as a state university.

"I majored in accounting, mainly because Larry and Stanley did and I liked bookkeeping in high school and thought it would be similar to math and accounting. My first job when I got out of school was as an accountant and now my job as vice-president of finance for MINACT is of course directly related. Someday I want to start my own company—thinking ahead—reaching for the skies."

Pearl went to Ole Miss in 1973, when Stanley and Gloria were still there. "I didn't go to football games or other functions. My social life was with my siblings who were there, and going home a lot. I was living in a dormitory. When I first got there I had a white roommate, but it didn't take but about an hour for her to be out of there. I just left my things in the room, I was scared to death, and I went down to Gloria's room, and my roommate could tell by some of the hair products or something that I was black, 'cause when I got back her things were gone. After that I got a black roommate.

"Ole Miss was a very good school. I don't remember having any problems. It was different from high school. Maybe the white kids grew up or something. Nobody was afraid to sit by me or anything like that. Sometimes I would still be the only black in a group in a class and the students were very nice. Of course it was nine years after the civil rights bill, but you know the strangest thing was two or three students from Drew were there and they were really different people. I couldn't believe it sometimes. They would come up to me and hug me and act like 'Oh yeah, you're from my hometown.' I would just hug them back and it was like all the past had just slipped away.

"I majored in administration, banking, and finance. Actually, my freshman year, my favorite subject was English and my professor was a nephew of Senator John Stennis. I didn't know much about choosing classes, and I guess we didn't really have a good counselor in high school. They should have looked at our scores on the ACTs and seen what we were good in to help us choose a career path. I will certainly do differently with my children. So when I got there, I think I just went into business because Gloria, Larry, and Stanley had before me. But if I could do it over, I would see what jobs are going to be open in the market in the next couple of years and make a decision from that. Now I work in Oxford, at Mid-Valley Pipeline Company, a division of Sun Oil Company out of Philadelphia. I'm the office manager there—about twelve years now.

"I'm glad I went to the white school at a young age, in spite of all the bad times, because it helped me at Ole Miss. I was talking to a guy there who does research on the campus and he was telling me how blessed I was, 'cause I was in the top 25 percent of the blacks who came to Ole Miss—the only ones who graduated. And I know that going to the white schools in Drew helped. There really was a difference between the white and black schools. Not only the books but the materials and teachers. The black teachers at the black schools hadn't been trained in higher-level courses, so they really couldn't teach past a certain level. I remember when we first got to the white school, the teachers couldn't believe some of the things we hadn't studied in the black school. When I first got there, I didn't know sounds and they couldn't believe that I didn't learn to read by sounds. I think I just learned to read by . . . I guess I memorized or something. So I was glad we made that decision to change schools—not only for me, but because it helped other black children to come after us."

Beverly and Deborah followed Pearl to Ole Miss. Deborah also majored in accounting and since graduation has worked in contracts and grants at the university. Beverly was the only child who did not major in a math-related subject. She majored in journalism and in the spring of 1979, her senior year, she wrote an essay that described what had happened to her and her brothers and sisters after desegregating the schools:

Here I am, my fourth and final year in college. I am proud and I feel that I have every right to be . . . I look back now and see my beginning. I see that small shabby house where I was born as Beverly Diana Carter. I see my mother, Mae Bertha Carter, and my father, Matthew Carter. I see seven sisters and five brothers. I see the fields of cotton and soybeans that surround my house, and I see that old gravel road that toughened the bottom of my feet during the hot summer months. I see the cotton sacks I had to pull across my shoulder, and I hear my mother's voice. She is fussing at my older sister for not picking at least one-hundred pounds of cotton today. I look back, but instead of smiling, I want to cry. It makes me sad to think about all the things that I and many others went through to get me to where I am today. I am wondering am I going to let all this slip away. My parents have done all they can to help me have the kind of life they wanted but never had. Now I am about to be on my own, and it will be my responsibility to demand an opportunity to get the most out of life that I possibly can.

When Carl, the last of the Carter children, graduated from Drew High School in 1978, he wanted to go into the service right away. He was intrigued by the travels and stories of his older brothers who had joined the air force. A navy recruiter came to the house, but Mae Bertha told Carl and the recruiter that Carl was going to college first— he could go into the navy later. Carl received a good score on the ACTs and he, too, chose Ole Miss. A lot of the white kids from Drew who had started out with him in the first grade went to college only to find Carl again. He laughs at the memory of his unspoken greeting to them: "Well here I am, hello again."

Carl stayed in a dorm during his freshman year, but he had two roommates and found it hard to study and easy to party. His second year, Carl moved into a trailer where he studied more, but looking back he feels it still wasn't enough: "I had good preparation in math in high school from Mrs. Stancill, but my graduating class was so small by then—only twenty-six seniors. Most of the white students had left and the school wasn't offering much by then. We had to scrape up a class to get chemistry—about eight people. No foreign language, only eighteen credits to graduate, and no college preparatory classes at all. So, like the others, feeling good about my math, I majored in accounting. Seems like all the Carter boys wanted to either fly or do accounting or both.

"I went to Jackson to look for a job after graduation and this was an eye-opener as well—no preparation for job hunting. I looked for a whole year and would have settled for anything in the accounting field. I didn't want to go out of state because I had a family by then. When nothing happened in Jackson, I joined the air force for four years.

"I always knew my parents were very brave and that my family was unusual. I thank God every day that I had such strong parents who stayed together and tried to instill some values in us that we could live by. And my mom—even though I ran away from school and didn't understand it at the time—now I know why she told us, 'You got to stay in school and do your best, because no one is going to give you anything. It's going to be hard and then it's going to get harder and you're going to hang in there. Because the only way you're going to get anything is if you have some knowledge—something that no one can take away from you.'

"Now, Daddy was always the leveling point—to even things up. Mom was always getting on us and he was always the one that let us get away with a little bit more than she would. If she was real strict, he tried to bring it down some.

"You know, Mississippi got a bad reputation as being backwards, and when I go up north, if I say I'm from there, they automatically think they know more than me and that everyone from Mississippi is dumb and stupid. But Mississippi is changing a little bit—it's got a long way to go, but it's changing. Now there's still problems about treatment of blacks at Ole Miss sometimes, but that's happening on other campuses in the North and West and everywhere. You just got to stick in there in Mississippi and if you see something wrong you got to let people know about it and try to straighten it out. Mississippi is home for me and I want to stay."

*Sustenance and sorrow: cotton
ready to pick, Sunflower County.*

Twelve

We Just Left

Recently, when I visited Drew and Toledo to talk to the younger Carter children, I also met the five oldest Carter children, from Mae Bertha's "first batch," all of whom had left Mississippi as soon as they graduated from high school. I was interested in what they did after leaving the state and in their reactions to their family's choice to desegregate Drew's schools in 1965.

Edna Carter, born in 1939 on Belle Parker's plantation, was sixteen-year-old Mae Bertha's first child. She is now married to Johnny Threats, and they live in Kansas City, Kansas. They have two sons, Travis and Kenneth. Kenneth was born mentally handicapped, and Travis, who has always been close to his younger brother, has a Ph.D. in speech and language pathology from Northwestern University in Illinois and is currently teaching at Case Western Reserve University in Cleveland, Ohio. Edna recently returned to school herself to learn computer skills.

When she was young, Edna stayed with Matthew's mother, Maggie Griffin: "I loved my grandmother. She was my special person. I was with her a lot because she was by herself. She was right down the road—I guess it would be like a city block. I would play with the other kids all day and then at night stay with her. She was quite a salesperson. She sold candy at church and I think they would get it on credit—special customers she knew she could trust and who would for sure pay her later. And she sold insurance policies for some company—I think it was hospitalization.

"Then she and my daddy would make a crop together. There almost had to be a man somewhere for the plantation owner to let you have the land and the house to live in. So we would pick like a bale for her and then come and pick a bale for us and then pick a bale for her and a bale for us. And I think we did the same thing when we were chopping cotton. All of us would work in her fields and then all of us would work on our crops. And that's how we did it, we worked together to get it all harvested.

"I remember her kitchen, because she used to have ice in a cotton sack. She used it for a refrigerator, and she put her butter and stuff that would perish into bags and wrap it up with the ice and it would last two or three days until the iceman came again and you got another big fifty pounds of ice and started wrapping again. I think Naomi reminds me a lot of my grandmother. And then Tom Rushing took over and he didn't want my grandmother anymore so she moved up to Shelby with her daughter, Alice. That's where Grandmother was when she died in 1956. Then Alice died not long after her mother, in 1964, so there aren't many of my daddy's folks around.

"I don't know how much education Maggie had, but I do know that all of my daddy's people, even his grandmother—my great-grandmother—Lucy Scott, cared about it. See, I knew my great-grandmother too. She was living with Aunt Annie at Belle Parker's and there was something wrong with her leg, so she used a cane all the time—I just remember her sitting in the chair with that cane and then going in the kitchen with her cane and cooking. She died in 1960 or 1961—a lot later than most of her children. As I was saying, they all could read and write—many people in that age group couldn't. And of course my other grandmother, Luvenia, even went off to school, so we got the importance of education from both sides.

"There were always books around our house when I think back. My grandmother Maggie would teach us to read words from the Bible and from song books that she had ordered along with the Sunday school literature. She would let us look at the books as long as we took care of them and didn't 'throw them around like some people.' And my mother read to us too and told us wonderful stories that I always wished I could tell like she did. And I remember my father buying the *Pittsburgh Courier* for a dime from a black lady in Merigold.

"I started out in a one-room school at Union Grove Church, went to the eighth grade in a two-room school, and graduated from Hunter High School in Drew. After the Supreme Court's 1954 decision in *Brown v. Board of Education,* they put an addition on that Drew school for blacks and gave it a name. When I was in the twelfth grade, we got advertising from the National School of Business in Nashville. I had read about people doing this, and I decided to go. Grandmother Maggie wanted me to be a schoolteacher, and she said any money she had saved was to get me into college. She died when I was in the eleventh grade and my daddy and his sister honored her wishes. I needed that three hundred dollars up front, and I got on the bus and went to Nashville. After you got there, there were jobs before and after classes to make money to stay in school. The people in the town knew that this college was out there and had jobs ready—mostly like house-keeping and baby-sitting and a few restaurant jobs. But I mostly took care of children for people who worked and needed help with the kids coming home from school at 3:00. So, I got out of class at 12:00 and I took the bus to go to these people's houses. I would clean up a little bit and stay there until they got off from work, and I got fifty cents an hour, which seemed like a lot of money because we got thirty cents for chopping cotton. So, what a raise—fifty cents an hour in a nice air-conditioned house.

"It was a great place—the National School of Business on Lebanon Road in Nashville, Tennessee. It's not there anymore. It had a dormi-tory, almost like a college, and I met people from all over the South. It was all blacks, and mostly females—maybe about a hundred females and twelve males that were taking accounting. Girls could take accounting too if they wanted. I wasn't very good at the typing, but I think it was because I was paying for something that I should have gotten in high school. Then I would have done much better. But I stayed and I was very good in shorthand. Then I left in 1959 with a stenographer's certificate.

"I met my husband-to-be, Johnny Threats, in accounting, but he was a year ahead and left in '58 to go in the army. I left in '59 and I came home in July, and then I went to Detroit to my grandfather's, my mother's daddy, Zeke Slaughter. He was sick and his wife, Mary [Florida and Zeke separated in 1944], wrote Mama to have somebody come stay at the house with him while she was working. I went in October and stayed with him until I got married in January.

"There were no hard feelings as far as I knew about him walking out on Mama and them. He was just Grandfather. I didn't really know him that well. He seemed like a nice quiet person and he told me some things he wanted me to know—like he was sorry he made a mistake and didn't know it until it was too late. That's what he told me—one day when we were by ourselves—just the two of us there at the house by ourselves. When I left in January, my sister Bertha took care of him for a while but none of us were with him when he died.

"I wasn't surprised when Mama wrote about putting the children in the white schools and about the shooting in 1965. My parents were active when we were growing up, and I was a junior NAACP member. So it was like a natural thing for them—the next thing, and I was a little afraid but I was really proud of them all. And one day I was reading—in Kansas City there's a paper, *The Call*—a black paper, and I saw this headline that said 'Ruth Carter.' I thought, I have a sister named Ruth, but I had no idea it was about her. It was a reprint from another paper, and they were saying that Ruth Carter is not a socialite and not a debutante but that she's a brave young lady.

"You know—we ran—we people who finished school in Mississippi in the early fifties—we just left. Maybe we should have stayed in the South."

BERTHA CARTER, Matthew and Mae Bertha's second child, was born two years after Edna. She moved to Toledo in 1962 and lived with her Uncle C.H. She had left Mississippi two years earlier to take care of her grandfather in Detroit, but she didn't like Detroit and welcomed the move to Toledo, where there were lots of cousins her own age. Her first job in Toledo was working as a nurse's aide at the Toledo Hospital. Married in 1965, Bertha has two daughters, Teri and Sherri. I talked with her in Toledo just after we had been to a wonderful party to celebrate Sherri's earning a bachelor's degree in education from Toledo University.

Bertha had a stroke in 1979, at the age of thirty-eight. She lost most of her motor skills and was told she wouldn't be able to work again. "But," she told me, "I was determined. I was mean and determined. I had made up my mind to go back to work and to go into the health field, and I wanted to go right then. They sent me to a psychiatrist who said I wasn't ready, and I said I was, and I started crying and carrying on. But I did go back to work in 1981. Now I work as a nursing assistant in a senior citizens' home, and it's the best job I ever had because after my own stroke I understand what the seniors may be going through.

"I didn't know about the school enrollment in 1965 because my parents didn't have a phone. I *was* surprised, but at the same time I was really proud—I had been going through some racial stuff right here in Toledo. But then I guess I wasn't so surprised, because Mother and Daddy always wanted the best for us. When we were growing up and wanted something, my daddy never once told us that we didn't need it. He never took the easy way out. He'd tell us the truth—that he didn't have the money. Then he'd do his darnedest to get the things we wanted. I have often wondered about having thirteen kids—all with different personalities. Yet Mother and Daddy still knew what to do. They weren't really hard on us, but they knew just the right buttons to push. I have only two kids and still don't know the right buttons."

NAOMI, THE third child and third daughter, is the only one of the first five Carter children to remain in Mississippi. She lives with her husband, L.C. Granberry, and their daughter, Lakeisha, in Cleveland, fourteen miles from Drew. She is in daily contact with Mae Bertha and takes care of her sister Beverly's children when Beverly is at her job at the Kroger supermarket in Cleveland. Naomi met L.C. when she came home from New York in 1965, and they became engaged. L.C. had two sisters who desegregated the white schools in Cleveland; the AFSC sent the Granberrys grants to help the family cover the additional expenses related to going to school for nine months each year.

I have talked with Naomi many times during my visits to Mississippi. I asked her once why she thinks she was the only one of the first five Carter children to stay in the state. For one thing, she told me, she married L.C. For another, she has mostly "good memories": "Yeah, that hot sun and picking and chopping cotton is about the only bad one. And even though it was segregated, you know, there is segregation everywhere. But what I like now is that children can play safely outside, you don't have to lock your doors, and Lakeisha goes to Pearman School, which is about half black and half white. We are zoned to go to a predominantly black school, but I just take her in the car to the other school. Things haven't changed much. Pearman, which has been predominantly white, still gets the best of everything right here in Cleveland today. It's sad because some other black parents here aren't even aware of this."

Naomi laughed when I asked her if she was surprised about her parents' choice of schools in 1965. "No, my mama knew that it wasn't really the color of skin that made white people want to keep us out of their schools—if we went and got the same education then they wouldn't have anybody to pick their cotton—that was the *real* reason. Mama knew it and I knew it. And we are a big close family and my brothers and sisters helped each other to stay in the school. I go visit and stay in touch with all my brothers and sisters out of state."

I also talked to Lakeisha, who was seven at the time. She said she liked to play the piano and watch television, that reading was her favorite subject at school, and that *Curious George* was her favorite book.

MATTHEW "MAN" Carter told me he wasn't the least bit surprised when his mother wrote him about enrolling his younger sisters and brothers in the white school: "I was in Guam and she wrote me about the shooting in the house and about the FBI coming down. I wanted to come home at the time because that was scary—they may have missed that time but they didn't have to miss and someone could have gotten killed. So I asked my supervisor about going home, but you understand Uncle Sam—I didn't get to go. I used to think how sad it was that the people who probably did the shooting were ones we had been working with for most of our lives—a lot of years. I guess they thought that shooting at the house would run us out.

"But Mama taught us to stand up for lots of things we thought were right. I remember when the money wasn't right at the end of the year after we'd picked cotton, my mom would say, 'Let me go down and see this person about how we need money—let me go and explain to him.' My daddy would end up doing it, but he was kind of slower, and he'd have to do it just to keep her at home.

"I can remember my mom coming home when I was twelve and bringing me my NAACP card, along with Edna and the other older children. In 1954, a white citizens' council paper came around saying that the NAACP had to be stopped because the 'niggers and the Jews' were trying to overthrow the southern way of life. We didn't know exactly what it was, but Mama was trying to do something so we could get a quality education and get off the farm. I kept that card with me all the way up—it was still current when I joined the military.

"Once, when I was about fourteen, I was walking at night and this white guy stopped and asked me did I know where so-and-so lived, and I said yes. And this guy turned purple because I didn't say 'yessir.' He said, 'Don't your parents teach you yessir?' I didn't know what he was talking about, so I got upset myself and I was ready to retaliate. But then I just gave him the directions to where he wanted to go, because I remembered that this guy used to whip people who worked for him. He loaned his vehicle once to a nineteen-year-old and when he didn't bring it back on time, he took his belt and gave the guy a whipping. Later my friends said, 'Matthew, you're going to get killed, because you were being disrespectful.' But we were just taught to stand up."

Man joined the air force in 1962 and remembers the racism when he was based in Louisiana: "I saw more racism there than at home. You ran into problems just sitting on the public buses. Or if you were walking on the street and something happened, you were an automatic suspect. I was stopped several times myself and questioned just because I happened to be on the street. There was discrimination in the air force, too—it was hidden but it was there. We couldn't get promoted. We were told we weren't qualified. They even had segregated buildings until right before I got there.

"And there's still racism everywhere—Arkansas, Detroit, Mississippi. Now in Detroit you might go three times for a job interview and still don't get it. At least in Mississippi I always felt I knew where I stood—no stabbing in the back—I *knew* I wasn't gonna get that job."

Man retired from the air force in 1983 after twenty-one years. He settled in Jacksonville, Arkansas, near the air force base, to benefit from medical and dental care and commissary privileges for his family. His wife, Zettie, another Granberry, is from Cleveland, Mississippi, and is Naomi's sister-in-law. It was Zettie and her sister, Lillian, who were among the first black children to desegregate the white schools in Cleveland. Man and Zettie have three sons, Matthew, Jr., Cedric, and Kevin. Man has degrees in computer science and in accounting and business administration, and for the past seven years he has worked for the State Department of Human Services. He began in the Division of Children's Medical Services and is now staff manager in the Office of Long-Term Care.

Matthew never did get to fly a fighter plane, but he has a private pilot's license and is also licensed as an aircraft mechanic by the FAA. He takes great pleasure in flying his sons on short trips and to the beach.

JOHN CAESAR Carter (J.C.), the fifth child, was born on one of Tom Rushing's plantations in Bolivar County, outside of Cleveland, Mississippi, in 1945. He lives now in Lake Charles, Louisiana, with his wife, Carol, two sons, John, Jr., and James, and a daughter, Chardá. He has children from previous marriages in Arizona and Mississippi. I was in Drew when he and his family came to visit his mother in July 1991, and I asked him about leaving Mississippi when he was eighteen.

"I can clearly remember that I just wanted out of the cotton fields," he told me. "I made up my mind that I was going in the air force and that would be my career. I looked in the encyclopedia when I was in school one day and read about the air force and said I was going to join. My older brother, Man, joined, but not at the time I decided to. I think I decided even before him. But when he came home from basic training, he told me how it was like a real job. So I graduated from Hunter High School in 1963 at seventeen and joined the air force in 1964.

"Then I lived here in '68 and '69 when I got out of the service and worked in the ceramic tile place in Cleveland. I wasn't making much money, so I decided to go back to school and ended up in Lake Charles in aircraft mechanics school—that's what I did in the service—and I never came back from Lake Charles. I could use the G.I. Bill, so it was '73 by the time I finished up. Also, the place I'm working now was asked to hire a certain number of blacks, so people were going around to schools and recruiting the best blacks they could get. By then, I was in auto mechanics school and the supervisor from the aircraft mechanics school suggested that I would be good for work at their plant— now Citgo Petroleum—and I've been there since '73. Right now I'm a heavy-equipment operator and I'll probably stay there 'til I retire.

"I was in the service when my parents put the seven children in the white school. Mama wrote me about it. I remember the secondhand buses and books and that always bothered me, and I knew it bothered my parents. So I wasn't really surprised by my parents' decision in 1965. My mom has been outspoken as long as I can remember."

J.C. reminded me of Mae Bertha in the clarity and straightforward manner of his replies to my questions about changes in Mississippi: "There's plenty of changes now. Mississippi is more peaceful. Maybe they don't teach the kids to hate as much. I can remember the time when we would go in a store, we'd have to lay our money on the counter instead of handing it to people. They didn't want to touch black people's hands, I suppose. But since we're on the subject, my opinion about the whole thing is that the people in America should just call each other Americans and get off this black and white issue, and teach their kids to come up that way.

"And you know, we had no business being in the Gulf War, for the first part. The next part is I don't see how our president can ask black people to go over there when he's vetoed the civil rights bill. When there's a war, as far as I'm concerned, it's a war for the rich. The only reason America was over there was to protect those rich oil companies. They weren't concerned about the poor people over there—they don't even care about the poor people *here*. And George Bush didn't care if blacks thought he was a terrible president because he didn't count us as people anyway. Unless you're one of the people who has all the money, he wasn't including you when he speaks of 'freedom.'

"All of the problems in the black community go hand in hand. Lack of education is the key. No education, no jobs; no jobs, no money— take drugs to forget, or deal drugs to make some money and get the things you never had."

There was sadness in the voices of the five older Carter children as they spoke about why they "just left." As Man said to me: "It's too bad when you're only seventeen or eighteen years old and have to leave a mother and daddy and little brothers and sisters that you love and your home place because you know it's the only way out of the cotton fields. No matter what success or good life we finally found, we felt we had no choice—we *had* to leave. We had no way of knowing that freedom was just around the corner."

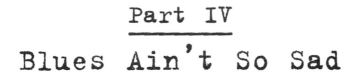

Part IV

Blues Ain't So Sad

Mae Bertha Carter, 1994.

Mrs. Carter (center) receives Award of Distinction,
University of Mississippi, 1993. James Earl Jones to her right.

Thirteen

Can't Touch This

By the early 1970s, Mae Bertha was feeling much less vulnerable to white community pressure and intimidation. She and Matthew were both in paying Head Start jobs, the public schools were thoroughly integrated, and all her children were doing well in the Drew schools or at Ole Miss. Other black parents were beginning to rally around Head Start and other federal programs that were changing their lives. At the same time, however, Mae Bertha was perpetually outraged over the seemingly endless deceptions and indignities perpetrated by the white power structure, particularly when her own children were involved. The family's sense of security and Mae

Bertha's personal indignation were a potent mix from which evolved political savvy and a talent for community organizing that have lasted to this day.

ONE OF the issues that really riled Mae Bertha was school board representation. In 1973, the Greenville, Mississippi, paper quoted her on the problem: "How can a man on the school board (DuBard) represent us (blacks) when he sends his children to the private school?" Mae Bertha got up a petition urging the school board to appoint black members.

"We are really mad now," Mae Bertha wrote me in her April 1973 letter. "I work hard going around to get the petition signed. We got around 350 names and the city board still appoints a white man. I can't understand it. Only 20% white children and an all white board with their children in private schools. They don't really care about our children being put out of school for minor things on a demerit system — you can only get 21, then you out for a year. You can get 5 for talking in class, leaving paper on the desk, for sneezing in the cafeteria. Something got to be done about all this nonsense. I bet about 30 children out for the year. But we are working hard after work to try to get an organization. We going from house to house trying to get members. There's got to be a change in the schools here, or half of the kids will be out of school and black people are ignorant enough now."

On another front, the court case *Andrews v. Drew Municipal School System* did prove to be a victory for the black community in 1973. The court held that schools could not fire black teacher's aides with illegitimate children on the grounds of "immoral conduct."

During the early months of 1973, the Carters were anxious about the various factions fighting for control of local anti-poverty pro-grams, including Head Start. The issue was further complicated by the move in Washington "to give the power back to the state," as Mae Bertha wrote. "I were listening to Nixon on the TV. He recommend the state take over the program that is now run from Washington. He rec-ommend the whole community action program be abandoned. I am sure if this happens, we better be looking for somewhere to run to. I am sure the people in Mississippi will be the worst off, and black people going to suffer. Send me the food stamp regulations."

By the beginning of 1974, both Matthew and Mae Bertha were still working regularly and the children continued to do well at Ole Miss and in Drew High School. With three children in college, though, the family's needs increased. Over the years, the Boulder Friends kept up their relationship with the Carters. It became much more than money for hot lunches or the monthly gift that had increased to one hundred dollars by 1974. The Meeting knew about everything that happened to the family and sent extra funds for summer school at Ole Miss, Christmas gifts, and summer expenses when Head Start was not in ses-sion and Matthew and Mae Bertha were not working. They took an active interest in the Carters' welfare and in 1974 wrote me that "it seems clear that aiding the Carters has been one of our most worthwhile if not the most worthwhile project that we have been involved in."

Mae Bertha reported in the fall of 1974 that "most of the white chil-dren have moved out of the school and going to the private school. I don't see how they can afford it with food up and everything. They are all poor. Just a few around here have money, but they are holding out. I believe education have went down since they left. We lost our good teachers. The children feel the same way."

In November, Mae Bertha sent me a clipping with a note on top—
"I just want you all to see what is happening here in Miss. This needs
to be stopped. To me this is Watergate." The clipping, from the *Delta
Democrat Times*, stated that since 1969 more than a quarter-million dollars in taxpayer money had gone for tuition for Parchman State Penitentiary employees' children to attend all-white private schools. While
technically legal under a 1969 state law, the tuition payments were
similar to payments that federal courts had consistently ruled to be
unconstitutional. The newspaper's investigation also showed that the
state had used thousands of dollars of Parchman general support
funds to pay for buses, gas, and drivers to transport children to North
Sunflower Academy, a private white school in Ruleville.

Despite its apparent unconstitutionality, the Mississippi law ena-
bling tuition payment for Parchman employees' children had never
been challenged in court. Written by Robert L. Crook, the state senator
from Ruleville, the 1969 law allowed up to sixty dollars per student
per month to be paid from state funds to any elementary or secondary
educational institution. Cleve McDowell, the only black member of
the Parchman prison board, was opposed to the tuition payments, but
pointed out how hard it is to change state statutes, especially those
that delay integration. McDowell, a Drew attorney, said that the "state
is surreptitiously underwriting the private schools, because we have a
concentration of legislators pushing these schools . . . money hustling
groups."

IN THE fall of 1974, the Ford Foundation notified the AFSC that it was
terminating the grant for Family Aid Fund work in the South. The
foundation felt that harassment of blacks who were attempting to

exercise their rights had eased and that the fund was now aiding families with general economic needs. The AFSC's Community Relations Division agreed that the racial problems in the South, though still serious, were no longer in crisis. The Ford grant was the only support for my project, though, and the AFSC decided to close it down. In February 1975, I wrote Mae Bertha and other families the AFSC had helped to tell them the program would be phased out around March 31, 1975, and that my secretary, Addie Ringfield, and I would be leaving the AFSC.

Mae Bertha wrote about how sad she was that we were leaving, but her February letters were also filled with news of the latest fight with the Drew school system—over a new achievement testing system at the A. W. James Elementary School, which by then was 85 percent black. Based on their test results, many black children were not promoted to the next grade or were placed in special education classes. Mae Bertha said in her letter to Jean Fairfax and me:

I am writing to see if you can help in this problem. We met with the superintendent and asked him if this testing system was anywhere else. He said he didn't think so. We asked if this would cause children to remain in the same grade and he said most of them. We asked if this would discourage the children to not want to go to school. He said maybe it would. We asked him if this wasn't grouping and he said that's what it was and it was called Special Education. I don't know any lawyers working for schools now. I think one motive for doing it is to keep segregation, keep children down for another delay. It's sad—one white lady even mad with them. She went to the office to talk to him about her child and what it would do cause she was failing a grade even though she got an A. He told her he didn't care about her child—the A grade was just on her level. Maybe you can tell somebody that can help us.

Jean and I contacted Marian Wright Edelman, by then the president of the Children's Defense Fund in Washington, D.C. She wrote a memo to staff members: "I'd like to help Mrs. Carter. She is one of the oldest and most courageous of school desegregation plaintiffs whom we should not let down. . . . I think we should consider some kind of independent challenge." We also called Rims Barber of the Delta Ministry and lawyers from the NAACP Legal Defense and Educational Fund in Jackson. Their investigation showed "Drew to have the highest percentage of 'special education' students in the state." Barber planned to meet with Mae Bertha and other parents to come up with a strategy.

I RECEIVED my last letter from Mae Bertha on April 17, 1975:

Dear Connie,

Your letter has been received and also Pearl's check for summer school. Thanks for everything. I am sorry about you leaving, I can't get you out of my mind. Seems like I lost someone in the family. I had somebody to depend on. Rims came to see me. We had a meeting with parents. The school problem is sad. Children are going to be retained. I hope and pray something can be done about it, if not our children will be failing, there will soon be a big drop out of school, about 90 per cent. I see it coming if this man don't be stopped. We found out the board didn't vote on the

grading system. It was done by the superintendent. I hope you
find happiness wherever you go. You shall have my prayers. You
be sweet. May the Lord be with you.

Love,

Mae Bertha Carter

This past year, almost twenty years later, I reread Mae Bertha's final
letter to me. I tried to remember how I had dealt with the end of a ten-
year relationship with the Carters' all of whom I respected and cared
for deeply. I have no record of a reply to Mae Bertha. Would I have
written, "It's been a pleasure working with you"? Or, "Best of luck as
you continue the struggle," or, "Have a good life"? Somehow I put my
relationship with the Carters and all the other families I had met
through my AFSC work behind me. Eleanor Eaton, in the national
AFSC office, was handling emergencies or unfinished loans and grants
in the South, and I heard from her occasionally about how everyone
was doing. In the meantime, I looked for work in Atlanta. In October
1975, I was appointed director of human services for the city of Atlanta
by Mayor Maynard Jackson.

Addie Ringfield, my assistant in the Atlanta AFSC office, found a
new job as well. Before we left the AFSC, we packed up hundreds of
files of handwritten letters from all of the families, along with our
answers to them, and sent them to the national AFSC archives. I must
have packed up a lot of feelings too—anger, frustration, wonder,
admiration, hope, and an overwhelming sadness. Perhaps that's
why, thirteen years later, when Mae Bertha and I spotted each other at
the Atlanta conference, we raced through the pews of Ebenezer Baptist Church and cried and hugged each other so tightly. And perhaps

that is why I cry even now when I drive by myself through the still-mysterious Mississippi Delta. My feelings are as conflicted as the forces that clashed in those small southern towns—the tragedies, but also the triumphs—and I am grateful that I was able to play a small part in the drama.

OVER THE past fifteen years, when groups have recognized Mae Bertha for her courage and endurance, she has accepted the accolades with humility, yet she is aware that her life is worthy of recognition.

I saw her at such an occasion in early August 1990, when she was in Jackson visiting Gloria. On the evening of August 4, Gloria invited her mother to join her at a "work-related" dinner at the Ramada Renaissance Hotel. It's a good thing Mae Bertha's heart is strong. The "business" dinner was really a surprise tribute from her children. The theme was "Our Mom, Our Best Friend." The only child missing was Larry, who was still in the air force in Turkey, but twenty-four grandchildren and ten great-grandchildren were there. Winifred Green and I felt honored to have been invited, and we both were close to tears the whole time.

Ruth was the mistress of ceremonies and presented her brothers and sisters and their spouses to the gathering of about seventy-five friends and family members. Each child, grandchild and great-grandchild wore a green T-shirt with the inscription "A Day of Celebration" on the front and "I love you Mom" on the back. The twelve children sang their version of a Stevie Wonder song—"We've Just Come to Say We Love You, We've Just Come to Say We Really Care"—and the grandchildren and great-grandchildren, ranging in age from one to ten years old, danced a choreographed number to M. C. Hammer's "Can't Touch This."

In 1991, the mayor of Cincinnati, Ohio, presented the keys of the city to Mae Bertha and declared April 9, "Mae Bertha Carter Day." The presentation was organized by BEKIND (Boosting Everyone's Knowledge, Integrity, Nobility and Dignity), and Reverend Maurice McCrackin spoke at the evening program honoring Mae Bertha. McCrackin still lives in Cincinnati and has remained in touch with Mae Bertha since they met in the 1960s, when Operation Freedom helped the family with expenses and clothing for the children. BEKIND was started by John Henry Simmons after he heard Mae Bertha speak in Cincinnati during an earlier visit. He later made a video for her entitled "John's Love for Mae Bertha." On the video he declares that Mae Bertha changed his life—that if a miracle can happen in Drew, then "we can mobilize around the schools in Cincinnati." He also tells Mae Bertha that she has touched no person more than him—"I was in the Devil's hands, and you reached in and pulled me out." He closes the video by reciting a Shakespearean sonnet to her: "Shall I compare thee to a summer's day?"

In 1993, Mae Bertha was selected as one of six African-American Mississippians to receive the University of Mississippi's seventh annual award of distinction. Five of her children, several grandchildren, and I were in Oxford for the luncheon and awards ceremony. When it was her turn to speak, Mae Bertha, barely visible behind the podium, was eloquent in her plea to today's parents to love their children and help them understand the necessity of education. She spoke of the shooting and harassment in 1965, and how, despite it all, seven of her children had graduated from the institution where she now stood honored and celebrated. How we loved the sweet irony of it all! She received thunderous applause, and James Earl Jones, another of the recipients, in response to the loud applause for himself, told the audience that Mae Bertha Carter was the "real hero."

But the recognition that meant the most to Mae Bertha was receiving the Wonder Woman Foundation Award in 1982. Marian Wright Edelman nominated Mae Bertha in the category of "Women Taking Risks." When Mae Bertha received notice of her nomination, she said to her children, "What's this Wonder Woman? I thought it was that lady that flies around on television."

Mae Bertha and Matthew were flown to New York City and stayed at the Ritz Carlton on Central Park South. It was Thanksgiving week and Mae Bertha said she will never forget "that big city with the beginning of the decorations and all the lights and it being so nice and cold and the mints and little cocktails by your bed at night in that hotel."

Mae Bertha told me she treasures the Wonder Woman Award for many reasons, including the memories of being treated so beautifully. But what she holds closest to her heart is that Marian Wright Edelman, "who is a famous woman herself and who knows so many fine and famous women all over the world, would remember me down here in Drew, Mississippi, and would nominate me, Mae Bertha Carter, no more than a third-grade education, to be a Wonder Woman."

The award recipients and their spouses first went to a luncheon that Mae Bertha remembers as "especially beautiful, where men in black suits served you something every time you looked around." At the awards banquet that evening, Mae Bertha wore a new two-piece navy suit and matching shoes and remembers being so proud to receive her award from "Archie Bunker's wife," who had made her laugh so many times on television. Eighteen awards were given in various categories, and the actress Jean Stapleton, as she made the presentation to Mae

Bertha, described her as "a woman who refuses to hide from danger and uncertainty . . . has a clear vision of right and wrong . . . and promotes harmony among all people as the goal of social change."

When a reporter asked Mae Bertha what she would do with her award money, Mae Bertha answered, "I'm going to hold it in my hand for a few minutes. Then I'm going to sit down and talk about it with my family, and I'd like to go back to school and maybe run for city council, which has always been all white men."

Winifred Green went to the awards banquet in New York and remembers how thrilling it was to see Mae Bertha honored by so many famous people, including Marlo Thomas, Joan Mondale, Judy Collins, Gloria Steinem, and Hugh Downs. At the reception following the banquet, Winifred introduced Mae Bertha to Franklin Thomas, then the new president of the Ford Foundation. When they walked away, Mae Bertha said, "Now Winifred, you can't be serious. You know there ain't no Negro head of the Ford Foundation." Winifred also remembers looking into the bar at the Ritz on several occasions and seeing Matthew sitting at a table with other husbands. She says Matthew usually sat with Eula Hall's husband, from Craynor, Kentucky, and Winifred can still see them clearly in her mind's eye—the black man and the white man, laughing and talking and sharing a bottle of Jack Daniel's and Coca-Cola. As they were all leaving to go home, Matthew came up to Winifred and said, "Miss Green, this is a very nice hotel, and the next time I am in New York, I think I'll stop here."

Matthew Carter died six years later on January 6, 1988.

Mae Bertha and Matthew Carter,
Drew, Mississippi, 1967.

Fourteen

The Best Thing About Matthew

On my first trip back to Mississippi in 1989, I asked Mae Bertha to take me to Matthew's grave in the cemetery at Union Grove Baptist Church. It was early May and the trees along the bayous were fuzzy with yellow-green early growth. The sprouts of cotton and soybeans and rice spread a darker green carpet over the black dirt. It had rained early in the morning and everything smelled fresh and gentle.

We bumped over the rutted dirt roads in my rental car and decided to take a detour to Busyline. Not a cinder block or a board remained of the Carters' house, and the huge barn had fallen in on itself. Mae Bertha pointed out a square plot covered with weeds and grass slightly different from what grew on the rest of the land. It was the flower garden that Matthew had planted and tended for her. We stood in the silence and remembered life there in an era that had also fallen in on itself.

Farther down the main road from Drew, we passed Belle Parker's. We crossed a rickety bridge over an almost-dry bayou overtaken by vines. On the far side was Union Grove Church. The one-room white frame building, which would burn a year later, had been the center of social life for the Carters for a good portion of their lives. Mae Bertha, her brothers and sisters, and most of her children were baptized there. The church had also served as the schoolhouse for both generations before school buildings for black children were built.

Mae Bertha spoke to a tall, thin man driving a tractor-mower in front of the church. "Morning, Sugar Boy," she said. "This is my friend from Atlanta come to see Matthew's grave."

I stood at Matthew Carter's modest stone marker. Between 1966 and 1975, when I was visiting the family regularly, I saw him a total of fifteen times. In the years of weekly correspondence from the family, there was only one letter from Matthew—written for him by Ruth. He had written in Mae Bertha's place, in the spring of 1966, when she had gone to Washington and Philadelphia. The letter, addressed to Marie Turner at the AFSC office in Philadelphia, read, "I am glad Mrs. Carter was able to visit with you. We are all very proud of her. All of us are doing fine. The kids are still doing okay in school. May God bless you and keep you and may your thoughts be with us."

I had come to think a lot of Matthew Carter. Often when I arrived at their home in Drew, Mae Bertha would be at work, and I welcomed the chance to talk with him alone. Matthew invariably wore khaki trousers and a sport shirt, and once Mae Bertha told me that he had never worn a pair of overalls because they reminded him of slavery. Whenever I was at his house, Matthew made me feel a welcome guest and never once treated me like a white lady from Atlanta come to check on the family's situation. He was, simply, a very kind man. Every time I met him I was struck by two things—his love of hard work and his deep devotion to his children.

When Eleanor Eaton from the American Friends Service Committee visited the Carters for the first time in July 1966, she reported back that she was

> much impressed with Mr. Carter. He is very conscious of his fourth grade education and claims he isn't very intelligent but he made more intelligent statements in the half hour I was with him than most people. He talked about how they used to be "good niggers and knew their place." He said their relatives and friends remind them of this and that there would be no trouble if they knew their place now and knew "how to handle the white man." Mr. Carter said people called them freedom riders and civil rights agitators and demonstrators. "Well," he told me, "all we are—citizens obeying the law, just like the freedom riders and civil rights workers, only our obeying the law will help our children get out of these fields. We have to show people it can be done and maybe they will stop being afraid." He also told me how it hurt him not to have farm work—that all he knows is farming but that he is good at that.

MATTHEW HAD finally found work as a teacher's aide in late May 1968 in the Ruleville Head Start program. His salary was fifty-four dollars a week. It had been almost three years since he had had a job that he could call his own, and those years had been filled with hopes built up only to be dashed. Following one of his many futile job interviews in Drew, word reached Matthew that a white public official had said he would die and go to hell before Matthew Carter ever worked in his town. It took the intervention of an outsider to get Matthew the Ruleville Head Start job.

Mae Bertha told me that "this lady, her name was Mary Coleman, up in New York I guess, and she would write me letters and send little donations to us. I would always tell her that Matthew didn't have a job, so she some way or another had contact with some people in Washington, D.C., and Jackson, Mississippi, and she called Jackson headquarters for Head Start and they called Charles McLaurin in Ruleville and told him to give my husband a chance, that he had to have a job. And Charles McLaurin called me at work and told me to tell Matthew to come on down that next week. Now you know I never met that Mary Coleman. You remember those two white ladies who came to see us in 1965 after the shots in the house? And they said that they would go back to New York and around and tell people about us and about our needs and what not and so she was one of the people they told. And she wrote us and sent us some money and then she helped Matthew get that job and he was so happy.

"After Matthew started to work, the older children were taking care of the younger ones after school but it wouldn't be too long because Matthew got off at 2:30 and picked me up at 3:00 in Cleveland and then we'd come on home. Matthew loved his job, he loved those children."

Matthew's pleasure was short-lived. Not long after he went to work,

Drew's justice of the peace called him to say that everyone knew he was working, so he would have to pay off his debts at Bob Pope's store or a suit would be filed against him. (Matthew repaid the debt over time and the suit was never mentioned again.) Also, after his first two weeks at work, Matthew and his coworkers lost their salaries because of funding cuts resulting from another scuffle among the various factions that were fighting over Mississippi's anti-poverty programs. Matthew and Mae Bertha joined demonstrations against the cuts at the county Community Action office in Indianola despite threats of job loss for all the marchers. When Matthew returned to Head Start in September 1968, he remained as a paid employee for seventeen years.

IN JUNE 1994, I met Mae Bertha in Jackson at her daughter Gloria's house. We were there for the thirtieth-anniversary celebration of Freedom Summer, and Mae Bertha, along with others, was to be recognized as a "Civil Rights Pioneer." During that visit, Mae Bertha reminisced a great deal about Matthew. "You know," she said to me, "before he retired, Matthew worked for almost twenty years in Head Start in Ruleville as a teacher's aide and the children loved him and he loved the children. He loved that Head Start, and he would get up so early just so he could be at work at 8:00. He felt more like a man than he ever felt in his life—to be off that farm and have a job and his money in his hand. He retired in 1985, and he died in 1988. He began getting sick in 1983. He was subject to blood clots, and he got a clot in his left arm. He went to his doctor who put him in the hospital in Ruleville, and they wasn't doing nothing for him but giving him pain pills. And he stayed in that hospital from one Thursday to the next, taking pain pills, and finally his doctor came in and said we got to get him over to Greenwood to the hospital. That doctor in Ruleville had called ahead, and when we got there they didn't even take him to his room. The Greenwood doctor put him right back on that sick wagon and said carry him right now to the university hospital in Jackson. It was a cold, cold night, but they said don't wait until tomorrow. We got on that road, horns blowing and making it on down, and the doctors all waiting for him in the emergency room, and they were so nice. The doctor told me there was no way they could save his arm—he'd had that blood clot too long. But it wasn't a race thing in Ruleville—that doctor was just irresponsible. And my husband was so good. I told Matthew he needed to sue him, but Matthew loved that doctor and always went to him.

"So I was all alone in Jackson, but I did call Naomi and told her about Matthew, but I also told her don't come down here, all the roads are slippery and so cold and icy. But do you know, she took the risk and came on down anyway. I said, 'Naomi, how did you make it?' She said, 'We slipped off the road one time but made it.' Naomi was crazy about her daddy. She stayed down with me until we brought him home. Then he went back to Head Start with just one arm until they retired him when he was seventy-five years old in 1985.

"Then, about a year later, he had a stroke. He was making up the beds one morning. I'm not good at making beds and I didn't like to. So my husband made beds for forty-six years. He was making the bed with that one arm, and he said, 'Mary, my arm's getting numb,' and I said, 'Stop making the beds, Matthew, do you need to go to the hospital?' He said his arm was getting more and more numb, and at the hospital they told him he'd had a stroke. He took medicine for circulation after he came home, but then he couldn't move that right arm—so he didn't have no arms. We had to feed him and bathe him, do everything, but the strangest thing—he could walk. And he could talk some but not plain. He could tell you what needed to be done. He didn't have no choice—we had to do most everything, but one thing about it, Matthew took it easier than I ever could have done. He just accepted it.

"Then in January 1988 we went to Jackson to stay with Gloria's son, Deidrick. Donald, Gloria's husband, and Gloria came to get us, and when they left us to go to Memphis everything was fine. Matthew was feeling a little tired, but he slept good that night, and then the second night is when he had the heart attack. Gloria had called home to see how we were, and at the same time I was telling her we were doing fine, I hear Matthew calling, 'Mary, come here.'

"I told Gloria, 'I got to hang up and go back there and see what your daddy wants.' Matthew said he wanted to go to the bathroom, and I got him up and we went to the bathroom and he let out two great bursts of air, hit that wall, went out, didn't say a word. When he was on the floor, the last thing he ever said was, 'Mary, help me get into the bed.' Then I was on the floor trying to do that mouth-to-mouth thing that I didn't know how to do, and then Deidrick called 911 and they came real quick. They took him away and told us to come in the morning—not to come out in the middle of the ice storm. It was like driving on glass. Cars slipping one way would go on that way. But I think they told me to come in the morning because they knew he was dead. And we called Gloria right back in Memphis and she had gone to eat. When she came back they told her, and she said, 'Not my daddy, I just finished talking to Mama.' Yup, fifteen minutes after she talked to me her daddy was dead.

"And I went to the phone and called Alberta, a friend of Gloria's, and I tell you, it's good to have friends—I don't care how many children you got, or how many kinfolk you got, you need some friends. Alberta said, 'I'll be right over.' And her husband brought her—it took about an hour because the roads were so bad and they lived out from Jackson. She came on over and took me to the hospital that night and we met this doctor and they had this room they come in when they want to talk to you, but I knew Matthew was gone. And I started hollering and crying and hollering and crying, and that doctor was so nice—he was white—he said, 'You want to call somebody.' I said, 'I got so many—in the state and out of the state,' and he said, 'Call as many as you want to.' Then we went to spend the night at Alberta's and she brought us back early the next morning, and J.C. came, although I told him not to drive on that ice. Gloria came back on the train, 'cause it was too hard to drive in the frozen rain. Then we went back to Drew and my children all came home and they all planned the funeral, 'cause I didn't know nothing but to sit up in my room. And I knew Edna was coming from Kansas and I could see in my mind, them going off the highway, and I told the children about that. And Larry he came and had to fly all the way to Jackson instead of Greenville because the plane couldn't land.

"So they all got there, but they all said they'd never been through any roads like that, even Ruth and the ones from Toledo. So I said, 'Thank you, Jesus.' Then we had the funeral the next day."

I asked Mae Bertha if it was hard for her after Matthew died. "Oh yeah," she said, "it's hard now. I *still* miss him and the tears come down like showers of rain. And when problems come, I think, 'Oh dear, if Matthew were here, things would be different.' And I didn't know how to do nothing. And that's where I made a mistake. I couldn't put my curtains up—they would be all this way and that way, and to nail a nail—I hit my finger so many times. I found out all the things that had to be done around the house that Matthew always did. I would say, 'Matthew come here and do this for me.'" Mae Bertha looked at me and we collapsed in laughter before she continued.

"But I miss him most to talk to. Let me tell you, sometimes there are things you don't tell nobody but you tell your husband. Some things would come up, and I would catch myself saying, 'I'll tell Matthew.' And then I'd say to myself, 'What are you talking about?'

"Because, see, when problems with the children came up, I would talk it over with Matthew—whether we should do this or whether we should do that. Then I didn't have nobody to help me make decisions. That was so hard and it's still hard. I miss him, 'cause I ain't got nobody to help decide what to do. Even with the grandchildren—I need to ask what to do sometimes—and nobody to ask. But sometimes I ask Beverly, and Beverly says, 'I think I'm taking the place of Daddy.'"

But perhaps the greatest tribute to Matthew Carter is the way his wife of forty-nine years looks when she speaks about him and remembers their life together. Sometimes she calls him Matthew, but most of the time she says "my husband." Her expression becomes dreamy and her voice soft and gentle, almost difficult to hear as she reminisces. She becomes more animated when she recalls some very strong statement that he made, some stand he took, or something he did for her or the children. Her shoulders straighten and her voice becomes strong and clear. Recently, I asked her to tell me the "best thing" about Matthew.

"Oh, that he never complained about anything—everything was just always all right. Sometimes, he'd be working, and I wouldn't have the food ready when he got home, and he would always say, 'I can wait.' And he never got mad at me when I'd fuss at him about being a farmer and not knowing anything else when we needed money. Matthew would tell me, 'There's nothing wrong with being a farmer. That's an honorable job.' He was that way when I met him and he died that way.

"But one thing more important was that he loved his kids, and he worked for his kids. He wanted them all to get an education so they wouldn't have to do like he did. He worked for that—he worked on Sundays and at night—he didn't go to church and didn't care what people said about him. When he wasn't in the fields, he worked at home—tending our vegetables, planting the flower garden for me, and the vegetable garden. I think he loved them children better than he did me."

Mae Bertha has a way of looking at me when she is saying something that she knows will cause me to react. That day I looked back at her and said, "Well, I don't know about *that*, Mae Bertha," and again we both laughed out loud.

Mae Bertha lent me a copy of the program from the funeral held for Matthew Carter on Sunday, January 10, 1988, at the Holly Grove Missionary Baptist Church in Drew. Matthew was a member of the United Methodist Church, but Holly Grove offered a larger space for the service. The family tribute read:

TO OUR DAD:

You slipped away before we had a chance to tell you all the things you mean to us. I hope you can hear us today.

"I never put it in words, but I hope you knew it, I love you."
—Deborah

"I want the world to know that you, Daddy, were always there and set a good example for us to follow in life."
—Pearl

"Whether I was right or wrong, you were always there to help me through it."
—Matthew

"Whenever anyone hesitated to do anything for me, I would say that's okay, Daddy will do it, and you always did."
—Gloria

"When I think of you, I think of being a kid at Christmas. On Christmas morning, without fail you were right there on the floor with us, sharing our excitement. Now I am truly grateful for that quality time, and hope that I will always remember to give that same attention to my children."
—Larry

"I didn't hug as much as some of the others, but I always came when you called because I love you."
—Naomi

"Thanks for waiting patiently in the car for when I had to attend after school activities, no matter how cold it got."

—Edna

"Daddy, I really did like your kisses."

—Bertha

"I realize it often seemed like it was my fault when the car had to be repaired, but that didn't matter to you, Dad—you never stopped giving me the keys."

—J.C.

"Daddy, when I find a man like you, I'm going to marry him."

—Beverly

"Daddy, I hope I can be half the man you were."

—Carl

"You always made me feel like Daddy's little girl."

—Ruth

"I like the kind of discipline you gave when I was a child, because it made me the man I am today."

—Stanley

We will always remember and be grateful for your fatherly motto which was "when my children are happy, I'm happy; when they are sad, I am sad; when they have a problem, I have a problem."

You were the dearest, kindest father anyone could ever have. You stood by us when we were in trouble, comforted us when we were in pain and sympathized with us when we were in sorrow. Your strength will always be remembered and your love always felt.

Your Loving Children

Carter children's tribute to their mother, Jackson, Mississippi, 1990. Beverly and Mae Bertha seated in front. In back, left to right: Stanley, Naomi, Bertha, J.C., Deborah, Matthew (Man), Edna, Pearl, Carl, Gloria, Ruth.

Fifteen

My Own Personal Religion

I 'm on my way to raise hell with the mayor," Mae Bertha said to me on the phone one spring day three years ago. "The board of aldermen didn't reappoint Beverly to the school board."

Beverly Carter was appointed to the Drew school board in 1986. When one of the five members of the all-white, all-male school board resigned in 1986, the black community realized it was a chance to get a black person on the board. "I'm going to write a letter of interest," Beverly told her mother. Later she explained to me, "I didn't really mean it at the time, because I just knew for sure that they weren't going to pick Mae Bertha Carter's daughter. I would be the last person they would pick. But I put my letter in just to show that there were black people interested. And believe it or not, I was appointed."

A member of the board of aldermen confessed to Mae Bertha that the board had felt it may as well appoint Beverly and make it official, because the alderman knew Mae Bertha would be at all the meetings anyway. Beverly was the only African-American on the school board. Several of the men on the board had been serving since the years when the Carters had filed suits against it over issues ranging from the dress code to workbook fees. Beverly was the lone voice on many issues such as the maintenance of high standards for teacher hiring and the public advertising of job openings as required by law. Mae Bertha and Beverly believe that her consistent questioning of board actions and her unwillingness to rubber-stamp board decisions kept her from being reappointed.

Beverly had majored in journalism at Ole Miss and returned to Drew in 1979 after graduation. She works today as a supermarket office assistant in Cleveland, Mississippi, and is also taking courses at Delta State University toward a degree in elementary education. She is a single mother of two: her son, Kerry, age thirteen, attends Hunter Middle School, and her daughter, Shayla, six, is in kindergarten at A. W. James Elementary School.

The only Carter child still living in Drew, Beverly has joined her mother in the fight for African-American political power and for improvements in the public school system in Sunflower County. In the 1950s, black people made up almost 75 percent of Sunflower County's total population of 56,000, but only 0.3 percent were registered to vote. The number of black registered voters has increased dramatically over the years, but the shadow of intimidation and violence lingers.

Although the population of both Drew and the county is mostly black, black voters today make up only 50 percent of the electorate.

"And just being registered doesn't make the difference," says Mae Bertha. "People don't know how important it is to vote. There's strength in voting. If the mule knew how much strength he had in his back legs, he would never let a man hitch him to a plow."

In 1992, African-Americans in Sunflower County scored a major victory when Willie Simmons was elected to the state senate, the first black senator from the Sunflower area. Simmons defeated Robert Crook, the white incumbent from Ruleville who had been in the legislature for twenty-eight years and wrote the bill in the 1960s that allowed tax money to be used to send white children to segregated private academies after integration. During Simmons's campaign, Beverly and Mae Bertha canvassed door to door and took people to register. Mae Bertha's home was Drew headquarters for Simmons. His election made him one of 42 black senators in the 174-member legislature and one of the more than 800 black elected officials in Mississippi—the largest number in any state.

TODAY MAE Bertha still lives in the house on Broadway that Allen Black arranged to buy for the Carters in 1966. Drew's population is now predominantly black and most people are supported by welfare. Main Street looks very much the way it did in 1965, except for the boarded-up stores, but it is not the same. Cleve McDowell, the first black man to enroll at the University of Mississippi Law School, hangs his shingle in front of a Main Street office. A public park sits on the other side of Main Street, where the railroad tracks to the cotton gins used to be. Every year since 1990, on the first weekend in June, the park has been the site of the Pops Staples Gospel and Blues Festival. Marvin Flemmons, white, born in Drew, and owner of the Music Mart on Main Street, has been the driving force behind the festival and finally succeeded in getting funding from the board of aldermen. Flemmons was listening to the radio one day in 1972 and heard "I'll Take You There," the number-one song of the year. He couldn't believe the song was by the Staple Singers, who were from Drew! He is a blues enthusiast and has pointed out to me where Howlin' Wolf, Charley Patton, Tommy Johnson, and other musicians gathered to swap stories and sing the blues.

Burner Smith, who grew up in Drew, serves as the first black chief of police. He told me his feelings on Drew's legacy of violence: "In some instances, you can't forget things like Emmett Till's murder, but you kind of want to put some things behind you and go on. Because if you dwell on this type of stuff, you get hostile. And I try to refrain from that type of thinking. We try to treat everybody alike." The ex-mayor "Snake" Williford, who now lives in Jackson but commutes to his insurance company in Drew several days each week, is always cordial when he sees Mae Bertha. In 1991, Mae Bertha received a call from Ruby Nell Stancill—the only teacher her children respected. Stancill asked Mae Bertha if she could name the Carter children as examples of her good teaching in her nomination for Mississippi math teacher of the year.

And there are other changes. Charles McLaurin, the SNCC project director in Sunflower in the 1960s who was anathema to the white power structure, is now the mayor's appointee as assistant director of public works in Indianola. Mary Phillips, a close friend of Mae Bertha, was the first African-American woman elected to the five-member

Drew board of aldermen. A black minister, Reverend Jesse Gresham, was elected in 1993. And a black woman, Sheryl Nelson, serves on the school board. In Merigold, the Hayes Cooper Center for Math, Science and Technology has been selected as the best elementary school in Mississippi and one of fifty national model schools by *Redbook* magazine. The center was conceived in 1990, when Cleveland school district officials called together parents, teachers, principals, and businesspeople to ask them to design a school where students could learn regardless of race, economic background, or family status. The school is a model for public schools across the Delta and serves almost five hundred students, 50 percent black and 50 percent white, in kindergarten through eighth grade.

But the scene of greatest change is once again the public school system. While the public schools had become almost all black after 1971, by the 1980s some white parents found they could not afford tuition at private segregated academies and their children began trickling back into the public schools. In the 1994 school year, 30 percent of the children in the Drew system were white.

As white parents realized the shocking state of the Drew schools, they began to join with black parents to work for change. One of the causes taken up by the integrated Drew Concerned Citizens Group was the failure to reappoint Beverly Carter to the school board. Janet Free, a young white woman whose two children are in the Drew schools, is one of the group's leaders. Janet's maternal grandfather was a white sharecropper in Sunflower County who taught his family that the public school system belonged to everyone. Christian duty, she told me, commands that people work together. When complete school desegregation came in 1970, Janet stayed at the public school and was the only white student in her seventh-grade class. Although her family was ostracized by the other whites in Drew, Janet and her three sisters never left public school and never attended private seg-regated academies. Now a bookkeeper in a Cleveland bank, Janet is married to Reverend Lonnie Free, the pastor of the Church of God in Ruleville, who himself stayed in the Ruleville public schools when they were desegregated.

The Drew Concerned Citizens Group has concluded that the major-ity of the schools' problems can be remedied with money, and its leaders are trying to learn how school tax money and federal funds are actually allocated and spent. One of the results of the group's work has been the formation of parent-teacher organizations at the three public schools in Drew. The three PTOs meet under the leadership of Rev-erend Eugene Anderson, a thirty-five-year-old black minister and cor-rectional officer from nearby Parchman. Investigation and advocacy by the PTOs have brought some improvements. In 1994, after three years with no new library books, some shipments finally were sent to the three school libraries. When parents complained about the ten-year-old band uniforms, new ones appeared. There are some almost-new school buses, and a new wing for the fourth grade has been added at the elementary school. But Mae Bertha sometimes feels that these are small buy-offs that do not speak to deeper problems. She wonders about some of the older white teachers in the public system who are "biding time just for the retirement plan, which they might not get at the private academies." She worries that school officials are not developing plans to put a stop to the drugs that are beginning to be a problem in the schools. In 1993, black parents were stunned when the competent black principal at the high school was fired by the school board and replaced by a man who allegedly had pulled a gun on some high school students in Cleveland who he thought were badgering some of his Drew students. But Mae Bertha and Eugene Anderson told me that the greatest underlying problem is the school board's constant resistance to a plan for parent involvement. "The school system has to realize that parents are the ones ultimately in charge of raising our children," Eugene Anderson told me. "The teachers and principals need and must have our input and support for what goes on in school time. I told the school board that the parents don't trust them. The parents believe the school board refuses to listen to them or allow them to play an active role. Our hope is that all the PTOs will stay under one umbrella to bring about change and then the old tactic of divide and conquer in the black community won't work."

Parent groups in Drew have received support from the Southern Regional Council's Community Fellows in Public Education Program. The council, the first interracial group in the South, celebrated its fiftieth anniversary in 1994. The program it sponsors offers training and help to community leaders who are trying to improve their public education systems. Mae Bertha was selected as a fellow in 1992; the following year, Anderson was selected with Mae Bertha's blessing. She said she appreciates his young and energetic leadership and is with him every step of the way in his drive for parents to become part of the decision-making process in the education of their children.

It still rankles the black community that several members of the Drew school board sent their children to the all-white private academies at the same time that they controlled the public school system. For Mae Bertha and the black community, this was the greatest insult of all—"those white men were spending my tax money and making all the decisions about schools where they wouldn't even send their own children." And despite the parent groups' efforts, William DuBard remains chair of the school board after twenty-five years, during which time none of his children attended the public schools. Following his most recent appointment by the board of aldermen in 1993, Mae Bertha and other parents voiced their displeasure to the aldermen, who responded that DuBard's experience and wisdom in school matters overshadowed any other considerations, and so DuBard will hold office again until 1997.

"Sounds just like the sixties sometimes," Mae Bertha told me. "But you know, we won back then and kept our children in the white schools then, by the help of God and hard work. Now we'll just have to set these schools straight again."

ON FEBRUARY 11, 1994, Mae Bertha and I sat in the dark in her house in Drew in the middle of the worst ice storm in Mississippi history. Drew had been without electricity for three days and would not have it for fourteen more. I had flown to Memphis two days earlier, rented a car, and set out on Interstate 55 South. The car rental person had warned me that the area was about to be hit by a storm and that Mississippi roads would probably soon be impassable. Since it was early morning I decided I could make the three-hour trip to Drew before the worst set in. Was I wrong! I have never driven in such terrible conditions, nor been as frightened. When I crossed the state line into Mississippi I saw that the enormous pine trees that line the highway were already weighted down with ice. Sure enough they began to topple and crash across the road. There were very few cars, so I was able to go slowly when crossing the short bridges, of which there must be a hundred over the small bayous on that interstate in northern Mississippi. Never had the "Bridge May Ice Before Road" warning signs seemed so relevant! The lack of traffic also allowed me to speed up in the left lane in hopes of dodging runs of ice-laden pine trees threatening on the right. Each time I passed a long border of trees and came upon a short space of open field, I would say, "Thank you Jesus!" I did not get hit, but a truck in front of me did, and finally, at Batesville, two trees blocked traffic completely and highway crews directed us off the road. I spent the night in Batesville in a cold, dark motel room that hadn't been cleaned, and ate cheese crackers and a candy bar for supper from the one Foodmart that had electricity. I tried to call Mae Bertha to let her know what had happened to me, but all the lines to Drew were out.

The next morning I ventured back out on I-55 toward Indianola. Since Indianola is the seat of Sunflower County, I figured there might be power there, and that if I got stuck again I might find a motel with a working phone. But Indianola had been hit as hard as every other place in the Delta. Power lines were down everywhere, trees had crashed across roads and on top of houses, and the library I had wanted to visit was closed. Tree branches and debris blocked its parking lot. I checked into a motel with some lights on and late that day spoke with Mae Bertha's daughter Gloria in Jackson. She said that Drew was completely without power, that phone lines were down, but that Naomi had called her from Cleveland to say that Mae Bertha had gas and heat and was staying at home and that everybody was okay.

Early Saturday morning I again set out for Drew, sixteen miles north into the Delta. The devastation I encountered brought tears to my eyes. As on so many other occasions, the large expanse of the Delta sky over the flat land and the far horizons made me feel that this was indeed the whole world. But that Saturday morning I also felt that it was an alien world. The gray landscape looked as if some gigantic herd had come roaring through, knocking down telephone poles and power lines and lopping off the tops of trees with their teeth. Smaller bushes or plants were bent to the ground with thick layers of glistening ice. Power lines on broken poles were draped across the narrow county roads between Indianola and Drew. Most of the houses looked abandoned, and there were no lights anywhere. I saw only two other cars on the trip. As I crept along on the black ice, I remembered Mae Bertha's story of the ice storm on the night of Matthew's death in 1988. I also thought of the 1932 winter storm when the snow was two feet deep in the Delta and Luvenia thought the world was coming to an end and fed her children sweet potatoes as they lay in bed covered with cotton sacks. I could not even imagine the fear and isolation *they* must have felt in those storms, outcasts in a society that was often as violent as the elements.

When I finally got to Mae Bertha's we embraced and held each other longer than usual. I was so glad to see her. I am happy whenever I am with Mae Bertha, and I felt a familiar sense of safety when I crossed her threshold. She had no idea what had become of me. She said she had not really been too worried, but that she had been saying a prayer or two. I thought about the infinite number of prayers that have emanated from Mae Bertha Carter over the years—the ones she said when Ruth and Naomi were in jail, the ones she said as she lay across the bed in 1965 waiting for the school bus to bring her children safely back home, the ones she said for her children trying to make it home for their father's funeral.

That night she lit an oil lamp and we found ourselves talking about religion, and I asked her about her life in the church. She began by describing the church on Smith and Wiggins Plantation that she'd almost joined fifty years ago. As we talked in the darkness, Mae Bertha held her six-year-old granddaughter Shayla close on her lap.

"I'll tell you about it," Mae Bertha said, "because my Grandmother Julia used to go to church all the time, at White Chapel Methodist Church on Smith and Wiggins. My family was Methodist when I was born. I was about seven when I started going with Grandmother to her church. I would go to Sunday school too, and then I would go back there to go to school. Sometimes we would carry big baskets of food— it was like a picnic but I think it was called a rally. We'd spread white napkins on the picnic tables outside sometimes, or on the inside on the tables and benches. My grandmother would bring cakes and sweet potato pie and chicken and dressing and everybody would eat and I can see it so clearly how good that food tasted to me.

"Now when we moved to the Deadening at Renova, I went to Rose Hill Baptist Church to Sunday school, church, and regular school. At Rose Hill they generally had a revival and the preachers would preach and we had to go to the moaning bench at the front of the church. I got saved at Rose Hill Baptist Church, but not baptized. My mother said I hadn't prayed enough to get baptized there—she wouldn't let me get baptized until we came over to Belle Parker's place and started going to Union Grove Baptist Church.

"We would go to Union Grove for Sunday school, for the Baptist youth group, and for entertainment like 'fish in the wilderness,' where you would put little toys and stuff in the middle and then you would pay to take a pole and go fishing. Then we did a lot of courting at the church, and your boyfriend would walk you home in the moonlight.

"Then when I was about twelve years old, I went to praying and praying and one day I went to the moaning bench at Union Grove. All the sinners went to the moaning bench, and you got down on your knees and everybody is praying and singing, 'Dear Lord, wash us clean,' or, 'Tell the Lord I'll be home.' So then it could be a week for all the meetings, and they would tell you, 'Don't eat, go on a fast and pray.' That's when I was going to do what the preacher said and stop eating and went to Mrs. Belle Parker's house to churn the milk. I'd go early in the morning to churn and Mrs. Parker would tell me, 'Bertha, go eat.' And I'd say, 'I don't want to eat.' She would ask me why, and my stepdaddy was there and he went and told my mother, my brothers and sisters, 'Mae Bertha's getting to be religious.'

"So, that's what they told Mrs. Belle Parker. And Mrs. Belle Parker, bless her, she'd pat me on my shoulder because she always knew if I wasn't feeling well. She patted me on my shoulder, pulled up a chair, and said, 'Bertha, you don't have to do all that if you want to be added to the church. You just go there and tell them you want to join the church and you get baptized. You don't have to do without eating, you know.'

"But I was so into that religious stuff and the preacher told us that you got to see a sign that God is going to forgive you. So I would go down into the cornfields and say, 'Now Lord, give me a sign—let me see the sun shout,' meaning to jump up and down like you do in church sometime. And I'd be looking at the sun shining on the cornfield and it seems like I heard the sun shout. But if you look at the sun long enough, since I got grown I understand it, something about your eyes and the sun—it looks like it *is* going up and down, you know.

"So after Belle Parker told me I didn't need to do all that, I was so glad, and I went on and I was united to the church. And then I got baptized in the Sunflower River that second Sunday. I been going to church ever since."

When I asked Mae Bertha if her faith in God had been one of the strongest influences in her life, she said it was, "but not necessarily the church, just my own personal religion, since I was saved and baptized. Remember that I've told you about that kind of protective covering came over me, like when we were down at the jail? I don't know what that is, but I'm going to tell you. Remember you asked me was I praying when we were in Jackson and I was going to make that speech? I said, 'How did you know?' I *am* praying, you know, before I get up there. When I get up to say things, then something comes over me and it's as if this is right. That's what happens to me—something protecting me."

"But what about the sixties," I pressed Mae Bertha, "when you were so terrified by all the things happening to your family? You couldn't be sure bad things wouldn't happen. Was it that your faith and this personal religion you feel so strongly kept you going?"

"He is gonna take care of me, is what I know," Mae Bertha answered. "Then when we moved into Drew and my children started going to the Methodist church, we decided if the kids were going we would too. We started going as family. That church did the same— pray and praise God and ask for your money, but there's more to do than go to church.

"Now Matthew was religious, but he was not a churchgoing person—like him feeling every time they opened the door, he would have to be there. He would be home working but he believed in God and Jesus. He used to tell me he didn't understand the churchgoing people who would leave people in need, like the sick. Or if you were on the road with a flat or a broken-down car, they would go on by—those Christian people—and say, 'Sorry, I would help you, but we got to go to church.' Most of the time those Christian people is too busy—they just don't get their priorities right.

"And after we enrolled the children, no one from church—no preacher came to offer help. We did hear about one preacher from Drew who was going around talking about how bad we were doing out on the plantation. Now what kind of minister would hear about us and not think enough to drive ten miles out to Busyline to see about us and find out what was going on?"

As I listened to Mae Bertha, I heard again her fear, her sense of isolation and deep loneliness during the years following the enrollment of the children. I heard her anger at the injustice and betrayal. But most of all I heard the strength and faith that had propelled her thirty years earlier to stand on her front porch on Busyline and play the record of John F. Kennedy's speech about equal rights for black children to a hostile overseer trying to convince Matthew to withdraw their children from the white school. And I heard again her unswerving determination pledged fifty-five years earlier to her firstborn, Edna, that her children and her children's children would never know the bondage of the cotton fields.

"And you know," Mae Bertha continued about the church, "I never heard any one of them preach about that chapter of Matthew. I been waiting and waiting, but no. Jesus said in that chapter—don't know the verse, 'cause I'm not a Bible scholar—but I know something about the Bible. He said, 'When I was sick, ye didn't visit me, when I was in prison, ye didn't visit me, when I was hungry, ye didn't feed me, when

I was naked, ye didn't clothe me. DEPART FROM ME.' And the man answered, 'When were you sick and I didn't visit, when were you in prison and I didn't come see you, when were you hungry and I didn't feed you?' And Jesus said, 'When you did it to the least one, you did it to me.' Then He told about the man that did feed Him and He told that man, 'You visited me when I was sick, you clothed me when I was cold, you came to see me when I was a prisoner,' and the man said, 'When did I do that?' and Jesus said, 'When you did it to the least person, you did it unto me. COME ON IN THE KINGDOM.'

"That's my favorite Bible verse, and I didn't hear it preached. I was just reading the Bible and then I come to this verse. And then when I think of the race problem, I tell people to think about the Ten Commandments before Jesus came. Thou shalt not kill, thou shalt not steal. But when Jesus came, there was a new one—'a new commandment I give unto thee. LOVE ONE ANOTHER.' That would solve all these problems we have here in Drew and everywhere else. Talk about going to church every Sunday when all you got to do—LOVE ONE ANOTHER."

Mae Bertha's voice rose. I told her that maybe she had missed her calling, maybe she should have become Drew's first woman preacher. We were sitting side by side on the sofa in a small room at the back of the house. The oil lamp was on a kitchen chair in front of us. It was completely dark by then. Shayla and I went into the kitchen to check on some cornbread in the oven, a Mae Bertha specialty. When I came back in I saw that Mae Bertha's shadow was cast against the wall. Her silhouette looked so small. Then I sat back down beside her. Her creased hands were crossed in her lap, not in the usual way where fingers interlock, but in her own characteristic way—her wrists crossed first and her fingers intertwined sort of down under. It gives an impression of an unbreakable chain. Her head was turned upward, she was sitting erect, and the flickering light on her face reflected thoughts not quite finished.

"Now here's what you do with the love. I tell my friends and people who go to church all the time and sing that song 'Trust, Trusting in My Jesus,' I tell them I don't think they mean it. I don't believe they're trusting in Jesus. Because if they trust in Jesus like they're saying they trust in Jesus, they'd just come on down there to city hall with me to register and to vote. How far are they trusting Jesus, they won't trust him to city hall?"

Acknowledgments

F irst and foremost, my heartfelt thanks to all the members of the Carter family for telling me their stories: Mae Bertha Carter, Edna Threats, Bertha Huckleby, Naomi Granberry, Man Carter, J.C. Carter, Ruth Whittle, Larry Carter, Stanley Carter, Gloria Dickerson, Pearl Carter Owens, Beverly Carter, Deborah Smith, Carl Carter, Luvenia Slaughter, Julia Slaughter Childress, C.H. and Elvira Slaughter, Alberta Lusby, K.C. Moore, Lakeisha Granberry, Ngina and Tandra Whittle, and Sherri Huckleby. Although Matthew Carter had died before I began interviewing for this book, his voice is in these pages as well.

I am grateful to the many other people I interviewed who filled in pieces of the Carter story: Eugene Anderson, Johnny Stacy and Georgia Baughman, Allen Black, Ernest Bromley, Owen Brooks, Mari Ana Pemble Davis, Nettie Brown Davis, Marvin Flemmons, Janet Free, Arnester Johnson, Elnora Johnson, Leroy Johnson, Willie Mae Johnson, Jimmy and Ruby Langdon, Isabel Lee, Mel Leventhal, Maurice McCrackin, Cleve McDowell, Charles McLaurin, A. E. Moody, Mary Moore (Mrs. Amzie Moore), John Sidney Parker, I. G. Patterson, John Henry Simmons, Zoharah Simmons, Burner Smith, Ruby Nell Stancill, Bear and Janie Taylor, W. O. Williford, and Mike Yarrow.

In 1990, I spent a year as a postdoctoral fellow at the Center for the Study of Civil Rights, Carter G. Woodson Institute, at the University of Virginia. I thank the institute and its staff for their support: Armstead Robinson, William Jackson, Pat Sullivan, Mary Rose, and Gail Shirley. Special appreciation goes to three other fellows that year, Adam Fairclough, Mary Ellen Curtin, and Penny Russell, who helped me so much then and who have continued to offer advice on the book as well as their friendship. Paul and Mary Gaston, Bill and Eleanor Abbot, Ray Gavins, and Mary Lee Settle also read my early pages in Virginia and counseled me as I began my research and writing. Joan Browning in West Virginia transcribed my interview tapes during that period.

Staige Blackford, the editor of the *Virginia Quarterly Review*, published my first written words about the Carter family. I am grateful to Nat Sobel for reading that article, for encouraging me to develop the story into a book, and for becoming my agent. Nat led me to the magic of my editor, Shannon Ravenel, who believed in me and loved Mae Bertha's story. Shannon's greatest lesson was that everything doesn't have to be in chronological order. What a freeing gift! Her unswerving faith and responsiveness, along with the energetic support of the rest of the staff at Algonquin Books of Chapel Hill—especially Bonnie Campbell and Robert Rubin—have meant more than I can say.

My thanks to the other readers of the manuscript who gave invaluable suggestions: Julian Bond, Taylor Branch, Clayborne Carson, John Dittmer, Jean Fairfax, Joanne Grant, Winifred Green, Melissa Faye Greene, Pam Horowitz, Cliff Kuhn, Mary Norris, Anice Powell, Fred Powledge, Pat and Glenda Watters, and Nan Woodruff.

The American Friends Service Committee has been vital to this project. Travel funds and training for interviewing came from its Oral History Project through the efforts of Joan Lowe; and Jack Sutters, director of the AFSC archives, has been of inestimable help during the whole process. Mary Norris transcribed and helped edit my earliest interview tapes with great enthusiasm and insight. Barbara Moffett, the director of the AFSC Community Relations Division for more than forty years and my colleague at the AFSC during the 1960s, provided resources and unfailing faith. I finished reading the book to her two nights before she died in October 1994.

The Southern Regional Council has been of great help. Director Steve Suitts found a travel grant for me, and Allen Tullos and Ellen Spears guided me through publication of two articles for the council's magazine. A Mississippi Humanities Council grant through the Smith Robertson Museum and Cultural Center allowed further interviews, and as a fellow at the Emory University Institute for Women's Studies I was granted access to the university's library.

Patti Black, Julia Bond, Nancy Boxill, Milburn Crowe, Ken Dean, Linus Diedling, John Egerton, Jerry Farber, Shirley Franklin, Shirlee Fuller, Jim Harb, Lloyd Henderson, Charles Hopkins, Jo Hunsinger, Donn and Sylvia Johnson, Thomas Kennedy, Donna Matern, Donna McGinty, Joyce Miller, Kay Mills, Virginia Sheppard, Martha Sterne, Jerry Thornberry, Mary Turntine, and Pat and Roger Zobel have all given me support in myriad ways, as have my friends and neighbors on Myrtle Street.

For historical background I relied primarily on three books, and I thank their authors: John Dittmer, *Local People; The Struggle for Civil Rights in Mississippi*; James C. Cobb, *The Most Southern Place on Earth: The Mississippi Delta and the Roots of Regional Identity*; and Marie Hemphill, *Fevers, Floods and Faith: A History of Sunflower County, Mississippi, 1844–1976*.

I am deeply indebted to my friend and neighbor Lisa Rogers, who roamed around Mississippi with me before we knew there would be a book and who has read and edited the material and endured with good humor its many stages of development.

Finally, for their never-waivering encouragement and more, I thank my sisters, Eileen Curry and Ann Curry, my brother-in-law, Enoch Hendry, and my brother, Philip Holloway, who died during the summer of 1994.

Index

Photographs